TOO MANY PROMISES:
The Uncertain Future of Social Security

Too Many Promises:
The Uncertain Future of Social Security
A Twentieth Century Fund Report

MICHAEL J. BOSKIN

DOW JONES-IRWIN
Homewood, Illinois 60430

The Twentieth Century Fund is an independent research foundation which undertakes policy studies of economic, political, and social institutions and issues. The Fund was founded in 1919 and endowed by Edward A. Filene.

This publication is designed to provide accurate and authoritative information in regard to the subject matter covered. It is sold with the understanding that neither the author nor the publisher is engaged in rendering legal, accounting, or other professional service. If legal advice or other expert assistance is required, the services of a competent professional person should be sought.

From a Declaration of Principles jointly adopted by a Committee of the American Bar Association and a Committee of Publishers.

ISBN 0-87094-779-6

Library of Congress Catalog Card No. 86-70430

Printed in the United States of America
1 2 3 4 5 6 7 8 9 0 B 3 2 1 0 9 8 7 6

In memory of my mother and father.

Foreword

At a time when the ratio of the nation's retired elderly population is increasing dramatically, the issue of public retirement policy has taken on fresh urgency. Although the recent short-term financial crisis in the Social Security system has been resolved, we cannot expect that its survival can be assured by resort to quick fixes. It will not be too long before the baby boom generation faces retirement. How can its future be safeguarded? Only by reassessing the problems and seeking reforms now, before the options dwindle.

The problems of retired workers have long stirred the concern of the Twentieth Century Fund. In the 1930s, the Fund established a Committee on Old Age Security and, in the 1950s, a Committee on Economic Needs of Older People. More recently, we supported research on the fiscal difficulties caused by ballooning police and fire fighter's pension systems and a historical analysis of the Social Security system, which will soon be published.

This study by Michael Boskin evaluates the nation's retirement programs in light of demographic trends and the well-being of the national economy. Boskin, an economist who had done pioneering work in this field under the auspices of the National Bureau of Economic Research, sought a solution to the looming crisis that would minimize the problems of the current Social Security system, especially its inequities and inefficiencies, ensure its solvency, and provide incentives for private insurance to supplement the national system.

It has taken time for his plan to evolve. He worked through a period of dramatic national and international economic and social changes, each of which had effects on retirees and the retirement system on which they so heavily depend. What has emerged is a sound set of realistic recommendations that would dramatically alter the system and the way Americans think about it.

Boskin has faced the difficult realities and asks us to do the same, but with the inducement that there is a way to ensure the future security of the retired—through a combination of private and public action. Whether or not his approach is adopted, his comprehensive assessment of the difficulties and his recommendations for reform should contribute to a needed reconsideration of national retirement policies.

M. J. Rossant, Director
Twentieth Century Fund

Preface

Social security programs throughout the world are being re-evaluated today in light of the rapidly changing demographic situation and economic constraints. Japan and the United Kingdom, to take two prominent examples, are considering fundamental changes in their social security systems designed to ease the financial burden of retirement income support from the public sector. In 1983, in the midst of a short-term cash flow problem, the United States undertook a major overhaul of the retirement and disability components of Social Security. It was designed to solve a disturbingly large long-run solvency problem. These reforms will hit progressively harder for succeeding cohorts of retirees and are due to be phased in gradually over the next quarter century. Unfortunately, these reforms, while a step in the right direction, are likely to resolve only a modest part of the financial solvency problem and do almost nothing to redress Social Security's other pressing problems of inequity, target ineffectiveness, and adverse incentives.

The twin pillars upon which the rapid rise in real Social Security benefits were based were the very high real growth rate in the economy in the 25 years after World War II and the poor economic status of the elderly. These two factors have undergone major changes, the latter for the better, the former for the worse. The absolute and relative well-being of the elderly has improved substantially in advanced economies. In the United States, real per capita income for the elderly now exceeds that of the general population, and many of the elderly have a higher standard of living in retirement than they did during their working lives. The incidence of poverty among the elderly has fallen from 35 percent to under 15 percent and is below that of the general population. Combined with the productivity growth slowdown of the last 20 years, there is a substantial case for slowing the rate of growth of real Social Security benefits for the nonpoor elderly.

This book is an attempt to lay out, in as dispassionate a fashion as possible, some important facts, trends, and analyses that should form the background for public policy designed to address these problems. These include documentation of changes in the economic status of the elderly, demography, Social Security financial projections, and labor and capital market analyses. The analyses lead me to a prototypical reform proposal: separation of the transfer and annuity goals of Social Security and a two-tier system. The proposal would directly link Social Security benefits and taxes, providing everyone an identical return on contributions in the major part of the program, while maintaining a separate welfare program for those whose earnings-related benefits are insufficient. Such a system is likely to be fairer, more target effective, and less distortionary of economic decisions than existing law and most suggested changes to it.

Acknowledgments

In developing these ideas and the technical research upon which they are based, I have been privileged to interact with and learn from some of the country's leading scholars—mostly economists—on this issue. While many of them might disagree sharply with my conclusions, I have benefited much from my interaction with them. I would like to thank the many researchers whose work I have cited in this volume and must express particular thanks to the following: Martin Feldstein, Victor Fuchs, Michael Hurd, Laurence Kotlikoff, John Shoven, Milton Friedman, Joseph Pechman, Joseph Stiglitz, Peter Peterson, Rita Ricardo Campbell, A. Lawrence Chickering, Marcy Avrin, Kenneth Arrow, Mordecai Kurz, Rudy Penner, Sherwin Rosen, and Anthony Pellechio.

I would also like to thank Douglas Puffert for invaluable research assistance and Rossannah Reeves, not only for typing the manuscript, but for making numerous suggestions for improving it and for seeing me through the arduous task of such a long project.

Some of the technical research quoted in this volume was supported financially by grants to the National Bureau of Economic Research from the National Science Foundation and the

Department of Health and Human Services and to me from the American Enterprise Institute on Public Policy Research and the Stanford University Center for Economic Policy Research. I particularly benefited from comments at the Stanford University Center for Economic Policy Research Koret Conference on Social Security.

Finally, and perhaps most important, this book would not have been possible without the financial support of the Twentieth Century Fund and the tireless efforts of its program officers, staff, and Director. Special mention goes to Joshua Nelson, M. J. Rossant, Beverly Goldberg, Masha Sinnerreich, Carol Barker, and especially Gary Nickerson. Ted Young helped organize the manuscript more coherently. Ms. Pamela Gilfond provided important editorial assistance and a much appreciated contagious enthusiasm for the project.

Michael J. Boskin

Contents

CHAPTER 1

An Overview

Public retirement policies in the United States are in deep trouble, and we are heading toward a crisis of unprecedented proportion. The potential economic, political, and social disruption this crisis may cause can hardly be overestimated. The financial planning of millions of citizens, intended to ensure a secure retirement, will be seriously impaired—perhaps completely undermined. Such enormous additional taxes may be required that the economy will be drained of resources badly needed for investment and innovation. Older and younger Americans will be pitted against each other in a battle over public funds. All this lies ahead despite the 1983 Social Security rescue plan, which only partially resolved the system's financial difficulties.

The crisis will occur for a variety of reasons, one of which is the impending dramatic change in the age structure of the population. Because of the post-World War II baby boom and subsequent birth patterns and because of the increasing life expectancy of the elderly, the fraction of the population over age 65 will double by the middle of the next century. Add to this a sharp reduction in the fraction of the elderly working in the labor market and a continuing depressed rate of private saving, and the result is that the aged will arrive at the eve of retirement having accumulated grossly inadequate assets to support themselves during their remaining years. Thus, we face the somber prospect of having to provide government financing for the retirement of a much *larger* percentage of our population for an ever *longer* portion of their lives. The full impact of this now readily foreseeable event will be felt early in the next century, beginning around 2010, and will last for several decades.

But it is a problem *now* because any sensible solution requires a gradual phasing in, perhaps after a grace period, of *structural* changes in our retirement policies. Abrupt changes will not solve the problem because they are likely to be economically disruptive and perceived to be unfair to those whose retirement options or taxes are changed virtually overnight. Complicating the issue is the fact that our political system, so geared to short-term payoffs, is singularly ill-suited to dealing with programs and problems that transcend the generations.

Recent changes in retirement policies have contributed to—rather than calmed—the impending crisis. In the past 15 years, there have been several major benefit increases and a cementing of "promises" of future benefit growth, providing fertile ground for demands for still further program extensions. The major pro-

grams—Social Security and Medicare—are now called entitlements and are paid irrespective of the financial need of recipients
with little concern about the extent to which the nation, as a
whole, can afford them. The Gramm/Rudman/Hollings balanced
budget act exempts Social Security while dozens of other programs' very survival is threatened. To ensure the financial solvency of Social Security, the largest peacetime tax increase in U.S.
history was passed in 1977. In 1983, taxes were raised again. How
many more times will the public withstand this process?

As tax rates rise inexorably to cover growing obligations, public confidence in the future of these programs weakens. Increasingly, young people question whether there will be any Social
Security at all when they retire. Current elderly* and retired persons are continually frightened by misconceptions about the possibility of reductions in benefit growth.

If we do not begin to make changes in our retirement policies
now, our options for dealing with these problems will be severely
limited in the years ahead, and the likelihood of economic disruption and political divisiveness will increase. Despite the severity of
the situation, there is, as yet, no consensus on how to deal with
these issues. In part, this is because the magnitude, the causes,
and the consequences of the problem have been obfuscated. In
part, it is because of the failure to confront the fact that, despite
considerable achievements, our national retirement policies are
not well designed to meet the intended goals. Merely tinkering
with the tax rates and making minor changes in the benefits will
perpetuate an inequitable, inefficient, and insolvent public retirement system for decades to come.

A BROADER PERSPECTIVE

While the financial plight of the elderly often receives public attention, little thought is given to how policies designed to protect
the elderly affect the rest of the population. Nevertheless, policies
affecting the well-being of the elderly, especially those influenc-
ing the retirement decisions of the elderly—such as the level and
growth of Social Security benefits, payroll tax rates, mandatory

---

* Throughout this volume, the term *elderly* will be used to refer to persons
in their 60s or older, since this is standard usage. It is perhaps becoming too
early an age for the term, given gains in life expectancy, health, and income by
persons this age.

retirement rules, and the structure of health-care benefits—all have significant *general* ramifications on our economy. For example, government social insurance programs must compete with other programs—from defense, to highways, to education—for funding. Recent estimates suggest that, if outlays for the aged increase as projected, outlays for *other* groups and programs must be decreased by 41 percent early in the next century.[1] The availability of resources to finance future investment and research and development—the backbone of an expanding private economy—depends on our ability to find cost-conscious and target-effective reforms in public retirement support programs. Still another critical impact on the public at large is that the high tax rates necessitated to fund social insurance programs reduce incentives to work and thereby impair our national economic progress. Because Social Security and Medicare spending together constitute the largest federal government expenditure and because Social Security taxes are the second largest—and by far the most rapidly growing—source of federal government revenues (after the personal income tax), Social Security and Medicare play a significant role in determining general fiscal policy.

The state of the economy, of course, also has a direct effect on our ability, indeed our desire, to finance these social insurance programs. Benefit growth depends on our general economic performance. In a rapidly growing economy, it is both easier and more desirable to transfer resources from younger, wealthier generations to older, poorer generations through programs such as Social Security. In a stagnant economy, this redistribution of resources is less desirable.

And a slowly growing economy is roughly where the United States finds itself now. The optimism that prevailed in the first two decades after World War II—a time of greater-than-normal economic growth—has given way to pessimism about the prospects for future economic growth. Efforts are being made to restore an environment more conducive to higher productivity, but the results are yet to come. Our public retirement system, predicated on a more rapidly growing economy than has existed in the United States in the past decade and a half, is a "social contract" that is no longer sustainable in its present form.

While virtually all the countries of Western Europe have more generous social insurance programs than the United States, they are having increasing difficulty financing them. Not only are the benefits usually larger and provided over a longer span of time, but the ratio of recipients to those paying the taxes to support them is much higher. Payroll tax rates range from 25 percent to over 50 percent of taxable payroll. All of these societies are scrambling to try to find more cost-effective programs, ways to contain benefit growth, and incentives to increase income and wealth. Recently, for example, the United Kingdom, Switzerland, and Australia issued government reports suggesting major reforms.

PUBLIC VERSUS PRIVATE FINANCING

Generally, private markets allocate resources to their most desirable uses. When there are many buyers and sellers, markets are well developed and prices reflect all social costs and benefits, there is no case for government intervention in the provision of goods and services.[2] There is, however, the thorny question of the appropriate role of government in redistributing income and wealth. In an economy as affluent as ours, most of us would accept at least a minimal government role in preventing extreme hardship, whether temporary or permanent, especially when the misfortune is due to unavoidable circumstances. Thus, public programs expressly designed to assist the elderly may be thought of as reasonable and fair.

There are those who argue that the elderly deserve no different consideration from other claimants on public funds. I believe quite the opposite, as the elderly are more vulnerable financially. In advanced Western economies in the 20th century, each generation has been almost twice as wealthy as the generation that preceded it. Also, due to disability, health problems, technological obsolescence of skills, and partial or complete retirement, the potential income of the elderly generally fades. Finally, the elderly have a relatively short remaining work life and therefore fewer opportunities to adjust to rapidly changing economic circumstances. For example, the elderly have little time left to retrain and retool should there be a rapid shift in demand away from employment in a particular industry. Nor would they have sufficient time to rebuild a retirement asset portfolio that has been decimated by unexpected accelerations in the rate of inflation.

The fact that the elderly are at a disadvantage, as compared to the general population, is undoubtedly a major impetus behind the many public and private programs of assistance to the aged that exist in most societies. Nonetheless, the elderly are, and will continue to be, an enormously heterogeneous group in terms of their net assets, opportunities for continued work, support from family members, health, and so forth. While their more vulnerable position might be sufficient reason to compel antipoverty programs to pay them special attention, it does not justify massive transfer payments from the taxpaying working population to the elderly irrespective of need.

Still, I believe society should provide some basic, *minimum* compulsory support for the elderly. Public support can be justified on the grounds that private provision for retirement, and private insurance for contingencies such as disability and ill-health, while important, may be inadequate, thus putting the public well-being at risk. Some individuals, for example, may not save at all or may fail to anticipate or allow for unfavorable contingencies (in the expectation that society at large will provide relief through the tax and welfare system). Since society as a whole will be called on to come to the rescue, it has a stake in making sure that everyone is protected, and it is prudent to mandate some compulsory coverage.

Granted, there is no reason why such coverage must be publicly provided; mandatory private coverage, at some minimal level, would accomplish the same objective. But there is a major deficiency in private insurance markets. Because of large transaction costs and the problem of adverse selection of risk (the fact that those who are most at risk are most likely to join life insurance pools), private annuities (periodic—e.g., monthly—payments for the remainder of one's life) are not available on an actuarially fair basis (that is, at costs based on true probabilities) in our society. To protect against these systematically worse-than-average outcomes, private insurers must charge higher rates than would be actuarially fair if everyone were covered or else go bankrupt.

Because actuarially fair private annuities are not available, individuals saving totally on their own for their old age must strike a difficult balance between saving too much (in case they die earlier than expected) or consuming too swiftly (in case they live longer than expected). They risk living frugally and leaving an unplanned bequest or living quite long and ending up impoverished. Because of the uncertainty of life expectancy, they are vulnerable to serious mistakes. Social Security, on the other hand, protects the individual by guaranteeing benefits—i.e., providing an annuity—until death.

Still, private retirement plans have a significant role to play—
a role that is being increasingly taken over by our public retirement programs. In fact, while the original goal of Social Security
was to provide that minimum layer of protection or compulsory
basic support, it has grown far beyond that in terms of benefits
provided and types of coverage.

HOW SOCIAL SECURITY WORKS

Of the myriad public and private programs that provide financial
support for retirement and related contingencies, by far the largest is Social Security.* There are currently 36 million recipients of
Social Security benefit payments and 116 million covered employees. Social Security pays five basic types of benefits: (1) retirement
benefits (in the form of annuities); (2) disability benefits (in the
form of annuities); (3) spousal survivor benefits; (4) child survivor
benefits; (5) hospital insurance. In 1984, expenditures totaled
$236 billion.

Social Security is financed by a flat-rate tax—split evenly between employers and employees—of 14.1 percent of taxable payroll up to a set level of earnings. The maximum amount of earnings subject to Social Security tax—set at $39,600 in 1985—rises
with increases in average wages in the economy. The Social Security tax is scheduled to increase slightly to a total of 15.3 percent
by 1990. Social Security benefit levels are indexed to inflation as
measured by the consumer price index.

The Social Security payment an individual or family receives
depends, in part, on a formula that loosely relates benefits to
average earnings subject to payroll taxes over the working life of
the recipient. This gives the *illusion* that people are reclaiming
what they and their employer paid in plus interest. In fact, nothing could be further from the truth. Current taxes are used to
fund current benefits. That is, the $236 billion or so being paid
out in Old-Age, Survivors, Disability, and Hospital Insurance

---

* In addition to Social Security and its related programs, civil service retirement programs, state and local government retirement programs, military retirement programs, railroad retirement programs, and many private pensions,
private savings, and private insurance policies and programs play an integral
part in financing the retirement of elderly Americans. The extensiveness of
Social Security, however, requires that many of these other programs adapt to
the Social Security system of benefits and taxes. Thus my analysis of public
retirement programs will focus on Social Security.

benefits are paid for out of current tax collections, *not* out of the accumulation of taxes previously paid by the beneficiaries.

Today's typical beneficiary of old-age benefits gets back a huge multiple of what he and his employer paid in (including interest). I estimate that approximately 80 percent of what current beneficiaries receive is above and beyond any contributions paid by them and their employers (including interest). Looked at another way, the typical 1986 retiree would exhaust the benefits payable from his and his employer's contributions (plus interest) within about four years of retirement. Thus, despite the loose linkage of benefits to taxes previously paid, as a practical matter the Social Security system primarily transfers resources from the current generation of taxpayers to the current generation of retirees.

About 90 percent of the labor force is now embraced by the Social Security system. In 1983, coverage was increased by reforms enacted to resolve Social Security's financial problems. Prior to that time, for example, federal civilian employees were exempt from coverage; in 1983, it was mandated that all new federal civilian employees be covered. In addition, prior to 1983, state and local governments could join or withdraw from the Social Security system; now, once in the system, they may not withdraw. Also, effective with the 1983 reforms, employees of not-for-profit organizations must be covered by Social Security. The extension of Social Security coverage combined with the increase in the amount of earnings subject to Social Security tax has raised the percentage of total earnings in the economy taxable by Social Security from slightly over half, in the early postwar period, to about four fifths.

With these funds, the Social Security system has provided substantial financial security to the elderly and kept many elderly persons out of extreme poverty. Social Security retirement benefits and Medicare provide almost half of the retirement income of aged persons in the United States, up dramatically from about 30 percent only two decades ago when the total average income was much smaller. And the elderly are faring much better. For example, while in 1959, 35 percent of persons age 65 and over had incomes below the poverty level, by 1980 this number was a little under 14 percent. The average income of the elderly as compared to that of the general population rose considerably over the same period. Of course, the importance of Social Security to the total income of the elderly differs substantially by income and health status. Social Security provides the overwhelming *bulk* of income for approximately *one third* of the elderly population; a similar proportion depends quite heavily on Social Security; the remainder receive the majority of their income from other sources.

Overall, the enormous growth of Social Security benefits—approximately doubling in constant-value dollars in the past decade—has been a major contributor to the relief of economic distress and hardship among the elderly. It is, however, also channeling funds to those who could by no means be considered needy, paid out of taxes partially levied on low- and middle-income people.

THE TROUBLE WITH PUBLIC RETIREMENT PROGRAMS

Several interrelated problems plague public provision of financial support for retirement and related contingencies. First, there have been and may continue to be periodic *short-term cash flow problems*—that is, the expected revenues flowing into Social Security may be insufficient to pay current benefits for a particular period. Prior to the 1983 Amendments, for example, which rescued Social Security from this financial dilemma, the shortfall was estimated to be about $169 billion for the balance of the decade. While the rescue plan solved the immediate cash flow question for the Old-Age, Survivors, and Disability Insurance (OASDI) portion of Social Security, should a severe recession occur, it may reappear. Further, the 1983 Amendments did nothing to resolve the projected long-run deficit in the Hospital Insurance (HI) portion of Social Security, expected to begin in the 1990s.[3]

Second, charges of inequity and unfairness continually undermine public support for the system and maintain inexorable pressure to increase benefits for certain groups within the population. For example, working women claim that they are treated unfairly because of the existence of the spouse's benefit. The spouse's benefit, which comes under the regular retirement portion of Social Security, provides that the spouse of a covered worker may receive benefits equal to 50 percent of those received by the covered beneficiary, irrespective of whether the spouse made any contributions to Social Security during his or her lifetime. Thus, if the covered beneficiary had a high income, the spouse's benefit might exceed the level of benefits due an elderly single female retiree—or even a retired couple, both of whom worked—based on her/their own earnings history. Therefore, someone who paid Social Security taxes for an entire lifetime may get back less than someone who did not pay in anything. Further, many who are entitled to benefits on their own account find they will receive higher benefits if they claim the spouse's benefit. They therefore receive no return whatsoever on their contributions. Many other such inequities exist.

Third, the current system provides a *variety of disincentives to continue working and to private saving*, resulting in uneconomic decisions with respect to retirement and saving. For example, for those elderly who continue to work, Social Security currently "taxes" away 50 percent of benefits for earnings above a modest amount and provides an actuarially disadvantageous increase in future benefits.* Combined with other taxes to which these earnings are subject, and the dramatic increases in the level of Social Security benefits available, these high tax rates provide an enormous incentive for earlier retirement.[4] In addition, it has been argued that the promise of Social Security benefits decreases the incentive to save for one's own retirement and thereby contributes to a low rate of private saving in our country.[5] Since private saving works its way through capital markets into productive investment, earning a direct real rate of return, the substitution of Social Security for private saving may substantially reduce the nation's capital formation and level of income.

Fourth, Social Security (as well as other public retirement programs) faces a *long-run financing difficulty* of immense proportions. The threatened insolvency of Social Security looms so large that all of the other difficulties can be resolved only in the context of a sensible solution to this long-term financing problem. Prior to the 1983 Amendments, the gap between expected revenues and projected benefits in the retirement and disability portion of Social Security over the next 75 years was estimated to be on the order of $1.6 trillion (in inflation-adjusted dollars discounted to the present). To put it in perspective, this deficit was larger than the national debt of the United States. The 1983 Amendments allegedly eliminated this gap. I believe and will show that this assertion is quite mistaken. Worse yet, the deficit in the Hospital Insurance part of Social Security is *three times this large* (detailed estimates are provided in Tables 1.1 and 1.3). Were we to deal with the long-

---

* Although benefits are subsequently recomputed, which may offset this effect (see the discussion in Chapter 3).

term financing problem by raising taxes, we face the prospect of a Social Security tax rate of 25 to 40 percent.

Fifth, there is an enormous *political problem*. Politicians thrive on short-term solutions, not on postponed payoffs that require tough immediate measures. With 36 million recipients of Social Security benefits, most politicians will not risk telling their constituents that they have reduced benefit growth and raised taxes so that 30 years from now our economy will not be in a shambles and retirement income will not be threatened. This is a particular problem since the elderly vote in greater percentages than the general population and thus are given disproportionate weight by politicians. And the fraction of voters who are elderly will increase dramatically. If we do little until the baby boom generation starts to retire, we may face a situation in which more than half the *voters* will be beneficiaries of the program, demanding higher taxes on the working population to pay for benefits.

Another political problem may thwart attempts to deal with the long-term financial insolvency of our public retirement program. It has been assumed that the various piecemeal proposals passed in 1983 to solve Social Security's short-run funding problem will provide for a massive surplus to develop in the OASDI Trust Funds from 1990 through about 2020, so that these sums can eventually be used to keep tax increases to a minimum. But we have *never* been able to maintain a large surplus in Social Security for long because, whenever Social Security ran much of a surplus, benefits were increased.

THE 1983 AMENDMENTS

In 1983, in an attempt to resolve the short-term cash flow and long-run financial solvency problems facing the retirement and disability portions of Social Security, Congress adopted, with some changes, measures proposed by the National Commission on Social Security Reform. The 1983 Amendments, while an important step in the right direction and, historically, the first evidence we are capable of dealing with the problems, provides at best, a "25 percent solution."

The major changes called for by the 1983 Amendments are:

1. The taxation of half of benefits for individuals and families with incomes above (currently) substantial amounts.
2. A very small and gradual increase in the retirement age in the 21st century.

3. Extending mandatory coverage to new federal employees and tightening the option for withdrawing from Social Security for some other groups.
4. Speeding up some of the previously legislated tax increases.
5. Increasing taxes on the self-employed.
6. Some possible cuts in benefits, such as delay in the implementation of cost-of-living increases.

These provisions were designed to solve the short-term funding problem in the retirement and disability portion of Social Security (OASDI) under "intermediate" demographic and economic assumptions.[6] They should get OASDI through the remainder of the 1980s if nothing untoward—such as a major recession—occurs. But because the overwhelming bulk of the shortfall is in the Hospital Insurance or Medicare portion of Social Security, where the deficit is three times as large as that in retirement and disability, this package is *not* sufficient to keep Social Security as a *whole* solvent for very long. It will only solve 25 percent of the problem. In addition, if the economy performs worse than predicted, we will be faced with the dilemma of a tax increase or benefit cuts again in several years.

Another problem with the 1983 reform measures is that, while it was expected that by taxing one half of the retirement benefits of *currently* wealthy individuals almost one third of the long-run Social Security deficit would be erased, this is not likely to happen. Congress established that only the Social Security benefits of those with incomes above set high levels could be taxed. Currently only a small percentage of the elderly have such an income. But since these levels are not indexed to inflation, ultimately virtually all of the elderly will be taxed on one half of their Social Security benefits. It is not likely that Congress will sit idly by when this tax applies to middle-class retirees. But, unless it does, there will be little effect on the long-term Social Security deficit.

The anticipated reduction in the Social Security deficit to be brought about by raising the age of eligibility for full retirement benefits also is probably overestimated. This is because there has been a growing trend in such situations (especially in Western Europe) toward substitution of application for disability benefits for application for retirement benefits. That is, modest disabilities that, although unpleasant and uncomfortable, really do not prevent people from working are used as an excuse to receive preretirement benefits. If postponing retirement causes a larger increase in disability claims than anticipated, the long-run projected cost saving is indeed optimistic.

Finally relying on an enormous surplus to accrue between 1990 and 2020 in order to head off the need for major tax increases when the baby boom generation retires is equally unrealistic. Whenever a surplus has accrued in Social Security, either benefits were raised or new types of benefits were developed. Thus it is very unlikely that such a large surplus will be developed.

Given the above, the 1983 Amendments probably will not resolve the OASDI deficits, which comprise only a quarter of the long-term Social Security deficit. The amendments do almost nothing to redress the substantial inequities and mistargeting of Social Security benefits. They provide us with a little time in which to figure out how to achieve a more efficient, more equitable, and less costly system.

MAJOR PROBLEMS AND THEIR CAUSES

The 1983 Amendments did not sufficiently address the two major problems plaguing Social Security: long-term financial insolvency and the fact that Social Security provides the wrong kinds of benefits in improper amounts to people who did not pay for them. While attention has focused on the expected deficit in the Social Security system, even if the budget were in balance, we would still be saddled with an inefficient and inequitable system that transfers income in perverse ways.

To illustrate this problem, let us examine the first group of retirees under the Social Security system. Consider a man who retired in 1940 at age 65. Assuming average earnings and that the sum of employer and employee contributions to the nascent Social Security system was invested at interest rates then prevailing, this worker would have an accumulated retirement principal of $68.36, yielding a fair annuity, based on then-prevailing life expectancies, of $6.59 per year. But the actual average benefit paid in 1940 to a 65-year-old male was $270.60—$264.01 of which was a pure transfer, or welfare payment. Extending this comparison over the worker's expected life span would yield a present value of benefits of $2,962, of which $2,893 was a transfer. Thus, this individual paid for only 2.3 percent of the benefits he received.

While the direct transfer from taxpayers to beneficiaries is most obvious in the example of the very first group of retirees, a similar process is repeated every time Social Security tax rates are increased or coverage extended. There have been many mini-start-ups of Social Security since the origin of the program. Consider, for example, a situation in which Social Security tax rates are raised. Tax revenue collected from current workers will increase, and this extra revenue can be used to finance a benefit increase for current retirees. Thus current beneficiaries receive a new "windfall" since they never paid the higher tax rates being used to finance the extra benefits.

In order to make Social Security politically popular—which was essential to its survivial—the illusion was created that it was analogous to insurance despite the fact that there was no accumulation of funds from taxes to pay for benefits. This illusion is no doubt one basis of the widespread popular support for the program, but it is also a reason why it is so difficult to eliminate welfare for the rich. Of the $200 billion OASDI benefits paid last year, tens of billions of dollars went to well-off elderly individuals, including millionaires—well above what they and their employers paid in plus interest. Suppose our 65-year-old male who retired in 1940 had substantial income from other sources—namely family members or private investments. Was it equitable that 98 percent of his benefits were paid for out of taxes on the general population? Certainly not.

Another inequity occurs in the treatment of unmarried individuals who end up subsidizing those with families. In addition to retirement annuities, Social Security provides disability and survivors benefits and hospital insurance. But the need for survivors insurance depends on whether one has dependents. An unmarried worker has no reason to contribute to funding for survivors insurance, and yet he is required to do so.

Thus, our Social Security and Medicare system is really a complex hybrid of welfare and insurance. The overwhelming bulk of the dollars spent now—and in the foreseeable future—will be an *intergenerational transfer* from current taxpayers to current retirees, disabled persons, and those receiving hospital care. These benefits, in the main, are paid irrespective of need. But there is an intergenerational equity issue caused by the fact that family members of different ages pay vastly different taxes and receive vastly different benefits over their lifetimes. There is also, because of the tax and benefit formulas, an *intra*generational equity problem as well. For example, within any given age group, there is a transfer from two-earner families to one-earner families and from single individuals to multiperson families. Most of the benefits provided are not paid for, violating fundamental concepts of efficiency and fairness, and they can only be defended for truly needy individuals. Unless benefits grow much less rapidly than currently projected, taxes will rise substantially, and a battle is certain to ensue over *who* will pay for *what* benefits.

The major cause of the long-term deficit—Social Security's other main problem—is demographic changes, which will increase the ratio of retirees to workers considerably in the years ahead. Under a pay-as-you-go system such as Social Security, benefits grow in harmony with increases in the tax base. But when there are severe swings in the demographic composition of the population, there may be huge bulges in tax collections in one period and huge benefit commitments in another. This puts tremendous pressure on the system either to accumulate surpluses when the population bulge is earning the income and paying taxes or to raise taxes dramatically on the succeeding generation.

Consider, for example, what will happen when the post-World War II baby boom generation retires. The Social Security Administration's intermediate demographic assumptions forecast that, at the height of the baby boom generation's retirement in 2020, there will be approximately 50 beneficiaries of Social Security and related programs for every 100 workers (compared to a little over 30 beneficiaries per 100 workers now). The increase in life expectancy and the decline in labor force participation of the elderly adds to the imbalance between those who will be contributing to the system and those who will be collecting from it. If taxes collected now continue to be used solely to cover current benefits, then we face the prospect of gigantic tax increases to cover the same benefits for the baby boom generation when it retires, starts collecting Medicare, and so forth. Tables 1.1, 1.2, and 1.3 illustrate some of the tax increases that may be necessitated if benefits are not altered. Under the intermediate assumptions prior to the 1983 Amendments, the combined deficit of the OASDHI system over the next 75 years averaged about 7 percent of taxable payroll. In dollar terms, this amounts to a discounted, inflation-adjusted, 1983 value of almost $6 trillion. The deficits will be much larger in the second quarter of the next century than they will be at the end of this century or early in the next.

Table 1.1
Projected Revenues, Benefit Payments, and Deficits for the Social Security System Prior to the 1983 Amendments

(as a percent of taxable payroll)

	25-year periods			75-year period
	1982-2006	2007-2031	2032-2056	1982-2056
OASDI:				
Income	12.01	12.40	12.40	12.27
Outgo	11.35	14.08	16.79	14.07
Difference	.66	-1.68	-4.39	-1.80
HI:				
Income	2.86	2.90	2.90	2.89
Outgo	4.34	8.78	11.19	8.10
Difference	-1.48	-5.88	-8.29	-5.21
OASDHI:				
Income	14.87	15.30	15.30	15.16
Outgo	15.69	22.86	27.98	22.17
BALANCE	-.82	-7.56	-12.68	-7.01

Source: U.S. Congress, Senate, Committee on Finance, staff data and materials related to Social Security financing, based on 1982 Social Security Administration Trustees' intermediate assumptions.

Under the pessimistic assumptions, things look much worse. As Table 1.2 shows (last panel), a deficit of over 9 percentage points could result in OASDI alone. The Social Security Administration estimates that the tax rate could exceed 40 percent at the height of the baby boom generation's retirement unless we either increase the Social Security tax much higher than any recent proposal or dramatically reduce benefits. What is at stake is not only the Social Security system itself, but also the ability of our economy to generate funds for investment and to provide continued

Table 1.2
Estimated Income and Outgo of OASDI (excluding HI) Under Alternative Scenarios, Post-1983 Amendments

(as a percent of taxable payroll)

Scenario	Period			75-Year Average
	1983-2007	2008-2032	2033-2057	1983-2057
Intermediate:				
Income	12.50	12.95	13.15	12.87
Outgo	10.66	12.64	15.23	12.84
Difference	+1.83	+0.32	-2.08	+0.02
Pessimistic:				
Income	12.53	13.08	13.52	13.04
Outgo	11.44	15.50	22.73	16.56
Difference	+1.08	-2.42	-9.21	-3.51

Source: 1983 Annual Report of the Social Security Administration Trustees.

Note: The 1985 Trustees report estimates similar 75-year averages as follows for OASDI: income 12.94; outgo 13.35; deficit 0.41, for the intermediate assumptions.

incentives to work to those who will have to pay the taxes to finance these benefits.

Table 1.3 presents estimates of the 75-year actuarial balance of OASDI, HI, and their sum prior to the 1983 Amendments, under the 1983 Amendments intermediate assumptions, and under these assumptions modified to allow for indexing of the taxable amounts and/or dissipation of the surplus due to build in OASDI. Clearly, *only* if neither indexing nor dissipation occurs will OASDI be financially solvent over the 75-year horizon under the intermediate assumptions. And *only* OASDI will be solvent. HI will still be in deep financial trouble. The notes to Tables 1.2 and 1.3, which account for post-1983 Medicare cost-saving legislation and other factors, reflect the 1985 Trustees report. The long-run economic and demographic assumptions in the 1983 and 1985 reports are quite similar.

Table 1.3
Effect of 1983 Amendments on Actuarial Balance of OASDI and HI—Alternative Assumptions, 75-Year Period

(as a percent of taxable payroll)

	Pre-1983 Amendments	1983 Amendments as adopted, intermediate assumptions	Indexing of taxable amounts or dissipation of surplus	Indexing & dissipation of surplus
OASDI	-1.80	0.02	-0.60	-1.20
HI	-5.21	-5.21	-5.21	-5.21
TOTAL	-7.01	-5.19	-5.81	-6.41

Source: Author's calculations plus *1983 Annual Report* of the Social Security Administration Trustees.

Note: The 1985 Trustees report estimates somewhat smaller 75-year balances for the total system of -3.2 percent under the intermediate assumptions (reflecting Medicare cost-saving legislation after 1983) but -12.5 percent for the pessimistic assumptions.

It must be emphasized that the intermediate scenario used for long-range forecasts has generally been somewhat overly optimistic. In particular, the 1983–85 intermediate scenario forecasts may be overly optimistic on increases in fertility rates (assuming a large gradual increase back up to 2.0) and life expectancy gains (the Society of Actuaries, perhaps naturally, predicts much larger increases). While the intermediate scenario may be best for long-range planning purposes, it does not relieve us of the necessity of prudent anticipation of untoward events, even if such events fall well short of those underlying the pessimistic scenario.

A SENSIBLE SOLUTION

Many solutions have been proposed to deal with the critical problem of financial insolvency in our public retirement programs. But little importance has been attached to the disruption, divisiveness, inequity, and hardship that are bound to result from the suggested alterations in the programs and the taxes to finance them.

It is my purpose not only to analyze the nature, causes, and likely consequences of the public retirement program dilemma, but to propose a solution that will minimize the inefficiencies and inequities in the current system, restore financial solvency, and provide substantial incentives for maintaining private insurance and saving for retirement and related contingencies.

The core of my proposal is to separate our national retirement policies—primarily Social Security, Medicare, and their related programs—into two distinct parts. One part—sometimes called the annuity or insurance part—would provide actuarially equivalent insurance (i.e., identical returns for each dollar of taxes paid by everyone) for disability, catastrophic hospital care, and survivors and retirement annuities.[7] The other—sometimes referred to as the welfare or transfer part—would guarantee a minimally adequate level of retirement income for all citizens.[8]

Only by recognizing the dual legitimate purposes of public provision of funds for retirement can we begin to restructure our programs in a more cost-conscious and target-effective way, tightening the link between benefits received and taxes paid in the annuity function and limiting the vast sums spent on the welfare function. By dividing the existing system into a two-tier system and initiating cost-conscious and target-effective programs for each, it will be possible to get rid of the enormous inequities and inefficiencies that plague the current system now and that will only become worse in the years ahead.

The separation of the welfare and insurance functions of our national public retirement system would easily combine with private pension and insurance plans and might facilitate the adoption of other proposals made in recent years to eliminate specific inequities and inefficiencies in Social Security, Medicare, and other programs.

But it will take enormous political will and a tremendous educational effort to accomplish this goal. The cost of *not* acting, however, is immense. Ultimately, we will be forced to confront these difficulties head on; it is better to start to deal with these problems now so that reforms can be eased in gradually, rather than be forced into hasty, abrupt, and potentially disruptive changes.

With this brief introduction to the problems in this vital area of our economy and our public policy, and a hint at their solution, let us turn to a more detailed discussion of how the difficulties developed. Are the problems of Social Security and related programs largely due to profligate spending decisions? Poor economic forecasts? Dramatic changes in the demographic composition of the population? Each of these explanations has played a role, and we must examine them to understand the full depth and nature of the problems and their solutions.

CHAPTER 2

The Economic and Health Status of the Elderly

INTRODUCTION

The current generation of elderly persons in the United States is, on average, wealthier and healthier than any elderly generation preceding it. By some commonly used but misleading measures, it is even better off than the current younger generation. More significantly, the elderly are better off than they were, on average, during their working lifetimes. These statements might seem surprising, but I think the discussion and data presented below will demonstrate that they are quite accurate.

The health status of the elderly has improved substantially. The life expectancy of the elderly has increased dramatically in the past 20 years, and there has been improvement or at least no deterioration in most other measures of health status. There are still elderly persons in severe economic distress, but the remarkable fact of the 1980s is the enormous gain in the absolute and relative standard of living of the typical elderly household compared to previous generations. Much of this gain is due to large increases in Social Security benefits.

It was not always so. Merely two decades ago, the elderly comprised a disproportionate share of the poor. A substantial number of the elderly were exposed to potential economic disaster—for example, due to inadequate health insurance coverage and the possibility of enormous health care costs. While there are several reasons for their improved economic well-being, by far the most important is the enormous growth of inflation-adjusted Social Security benefits and the adoption and expansion of Medicare.

So startling is the dramatic improvement in the well-being of the *average* elderly person, and so poorly has this information been disseminated, that misconceptions abound. It is commonly assumed that many elderly persons are poor, suffer severe medical problems, and are in need of more assistance than they are currently receiving. But while these notions might have been true earlier of the bulk of the elderly population, today they are true of only a small minority of elderly persons.

The other remarkable fact about the elderly population is the substantial decline in their labor force participation. Combined with the enormous increase in life expectancy, this has created a large increase in the average length of retirement. Together with the substantial *number* of elderly persons and the growing number of "old" elderly (as compared to "young" elderly), a severe pressure is foreshadowed not only on the Social Security system's finances, but also on capital and labor markets and intrafamily, intergenerational social relations.

The combination of greater life expectancy, earlier retirement, and substantial improvement in economic well-being is the background against which sensible public policy on retirement, Social Security benefits, and the structure of Medicare must be made. If, as the data clearly show, most of the elderly are well-off as compared to during their earlier working years and many are well-off as compared to the general population, the question arises whether the current and projected structure of Social Security benefits is sensible in light of other pressing needs and the limited resources available to finance them.

THE ECONOMIC STATUS OF THE ELDERLY

Popular wisdom has it that most of the elderly are not very well-off (living at or below the poverty level), that their Social Security benefits are their only source of income, that they are much worse off during retirement than they ever were during their working years, and that they are disproportionately subject to economic disruption caused by inflation. But these conceptions are inaccurate. While some of them apply to a small number of the elderly, none of them is true with respect to the average elderly household. This fact, no doubt, will surprise many readers because, as late as the 1960s, virtually all of the notions were correct. But the huge growth of Social Security benefits, their indexing, the expansion of private pensions, the availability of alternative means of support, and the nature of the inflation and growth performance of the U.S. economy from the late 1960s to the early 1980s rendered the elderly the group in the population with by far the largest relative gains in its standard of living.

Nonetheless, it is not difficult to find summary measures that suggest that the elderly are still not very well-off. Among them, the "replacement rate"—developed by the Social Security Administration to answer the question, "What fraction of earnings does Social Security replace during retirement?"—is perhaps the most important. But this computation is enormously misleading. It is constructed in a manner that ignores fundamental features of our tax and insurance systems and the typical life cycle of earnings and income with respect to age. As will be seen below, a properly measured replacement rate probably *exceeds* 100%, on average, for the elderly population.

Before comparing the amounts and sources of income of the elderly with those of the general population and with those of the elderly during their earlier working years, it is important to make sure that proper comparisons of purchasing power are made. For this purpose, age-specific cost-of-living indices were developed to account for the fact that the elderly have a somewhat different expenditure pattern than the rest of the population. They consume more medical care, for example, and less food and transportation (see panel 1 of Table 2.1). Nevertheless, not only is the cumulative cost-of-living index for the elderly virtually identical to that for the general population, but in no single year did the measured inflation rate for the elderly differ much from that of the general population (see panels 2 and 3 of Table 2.1). Thus, the inflation of the past 15 years did not disproportionately affect the elderly's purchasing power—at any given level of income—as compared to the purchasing power of the general population.

The popular conception that inflation has affected the income and the value of assets held by the elderly more than the general population also is incorrect. John Shoven and Michael Hurd have pointed out that the inflation exposure of the elderly was less than that of the general population.[1] This is partly because of the indexing of Social Security benefits, partly because of the type of assets owned by the elderly, and partly because of other sources of income. For example, the elderly, on average, own a substantial amount of housing relative to the general population, and housing has been an inflation hedge.

In 1980, the average after-tax income per household member in the United States was $5,964, while the average for households headed by someone 65 years old or older was $6,299. There has been evidence of this same general phenomenon since at least 1970. While average income per household member is not the last word on economic well-being (children, for example, probably impose fewer costs than do adults), it is clear from the above that the elderly are not terribly different from the total population in after-tax income. On a per *household* basis, however, the average income of the elderly is much lower since their household sizes are much smaller; in the 1970s, the average household income of the elderly was slightly over half that of the nonelderly.

Nevertheless, real income per household has risen sharply for the elderly (rising about 23 percent from 1970 to 1980), while corresponding figures for the entire population show no growth. Thus, the elderly experienced a substantial gain in their standard

Table 2.1
Inflation and the Elderly

1. Major Expenditures: Elderly vs. General Population

Commodity	Age	
	Under 60	65-69
Owned Dwelling, Home	14.2%	20.3%
Transportation, Vacation	20.2	15.2
Medical Care	4.9	7.3

2. Cumulative Cost of Living: Elderly vs. General Population (1967=100)

Year	Under 55	65-69
1967	100.0	100.0
1972	121.5	121.9
1977	174.7	175.5
1980	228.2	228.8
1981	250.1	251.1

3. Average Annual Inflation Rates: Elderly vs. General Population

Year	Under 55	65-69
1967	2.40%	2.35%
1972	2.92	3.13
1977	6.66	6.80
1980	11.34	11.16
1981	9.58	9.73

Source: Michael J. Boskin and Michael D. Hurd, "Indexing Social Security Benefits: A Separate Price Index for the Elderly?" *Public Finance Quarterly,* October 1985.

Table 2.2
Relative Income of the Elderly
(Elderly/General Population)

Year	Income per Capita	Income per Household
1970	1.04	0.52
1973	1.05	0.54
1976	1.09	0.57
1978	1.06	0.58
1980	1.08	0.61

Sources: 1970, 1973, 1976, 1978: Michael Hurd and John Shoven, "Real Income and Wealth of the Elderly," American Economic Review, May 1982. 1980: Author's adjustments to U.S. Bureau of the Census, Series P-23, No. 126, August 1983.

of living at a time when the general population had virtually no gain at all. The remarkable increase in the relative income per household of the elderly in so short a time-span as a decade is presented in Table 2.2. (Similar trends have occurred elsewhere, e.g., the United Kingdom.)

But how have the poorest of the elderly fared? It is quite possible that while the elderly in general experienced substantial income gains, those at the lower end of the income scale did not. The Census Bureau reports that the total percentage of persons 65 years and over who are below the poverty line declined from 35 percent around 1960 to 14.6 percent in 1982 (see top panel, Table 2.3). Further, from 1979 to 1982, when the total incidence of poverty in the United States increased from 11.7 to 15.0 percent as a result of severe recession and double-digit inflation, the poverty rate for persons age 65 years and over actually declined from 15.2 to 14.6 percent. In the United Kingdom, a similar phenomenon can be observed; the proportion of the elderly in the bottom quintile of the income distribution fell from 35 percent to 19 percent between 1971 and 1982.

Also, the official poverty data include only the value of cash income. The enormous growth of noncash benefits, such as subsi-

Table 2.3
Poverty Status of the Elderly

1. Percentage of Persons Sixty-Five and Over Below the Poverty Line

Year	Percent
1959	35.2
1968	25.0
1970	24.5
1972	18.6
1974	15.7
1976	15.0
1979	15.2
1982	14.6

2. Poverty Rate of the Elderly Under Alternative Valuations of Noncash Benefits

Year	Official Definition	Valuing Food and Housing Benefits	Valuing Food, Housing, and Medical Benefits	Valuing Food, Housing and Medical Benefits at Market Value
1979	15.2%	13.4%	9.5%	4.3%
1982	14.6	13.1	9.3	3.5

Source: U.S. Bureau of the Census, Series P-60, various years; and U.S. Bureau of the Census, "Estimates of Poverty Including Noncash Benefits: 1979-1982," Technical Paper 51 (Washington, D.C.: U.S. Government Printing Office, 1984).

dized food, housing, and medical care, is not counted at all in the incomes of the poor. Thus, to the extent that noncash benefits are worth something, the official incidence of poverty overstates the true amount of impoverishment. A recent Census Bureau study suggests that, if a market-value approach were taken to evaluate food, housing, and medical benefits, the incidence of poverty among the elderly in the United States in 1982 would be reduced from 14.6 percent to 3.5 percent.[2] A somewhat less extreme approach, attempting to value what the recipient would pay for such expenditures rather than their market value, produces a poverty rate of 9.3 percent. Whichever of these figures one embraces (presented in the bottom panel of Table 2.3), the moral derived from them is clear: a smaller and smaller fraction of the elderly live below the poverty line, and the poorest of the elderly have some protection against economic recession and deterioration of their income due to inflation.

Thus, the bulk of the elderly have a reasonable absolute standard of living, not much chance of poverty anymore, and protection against major risks.[3] But still another comparison is critical; that is, how well-off are the elderly during retirement as compared to during their working years? This question is perhaps the single *most important* issue in addressing the adequacy, the level, the structure, and the growth of Social Security and Medicare benefits.

To give a first cut at answering this question, the Social Security Administration employs the concept of a "replacement rate." The traditional replacement rate calculation reports the ratio of Social Security benefits (and/or total income) during retirement to the average income of the 3 years of highest earnings in the 10 years prior to retirement. Table 2.4 presents these replacement rates by household type and by average income level. Clearly, the Social Security system *appears* to be replacing only a modest fraction of earnings. But the benefit formula is tilted to favor those with lower than average incomes; therefore the replacement rates for the lowest income groups are highest. While discussions about Social Security reform usually focus on these numbers, they suffer from a number of defects.

First, it is extremely difficult to compare the well-being of a couple after retirement to their standard of living during their working life. Arriving at some measure of comparable income flows is tricky; the data are not always readily available, and their interpretation can be difficult. For example, until 1984, Social Security benefits were untaxed, whereas average earnings—included in the denominator in the typical replacement rate calculation—were taxed.

A second problem with replacement rate calculations is that, given the usual age-earnings profile, the highest 3 years of earnings in the 10 years prior to retirement are likely dramatically to

Table 2.4
Replacement Rates* Relative To Highest Three Years Average Earnings, 1979

	Social Security Benefits	Total Income
By Household Type:		
Married Couples	39.84%	72.54%
Widows	33.17	58.77
By Average Annual Income Class:		
under $7,500	58.78	95.91
$7,500-12,499	43.62	73.21
$12,500-19,999	32.04	57.89
$20,000-29,999	24.05	49.92
$30,000-49,999	17.74	53.91
$50,000+	6.83	33.51

* Based on author's calculations from Longitudinal Retirement History Survey. Data are price indexed, any year of retirement, highest three years of earnings, unadjusted for taxes, children, and risk.

overstate the average *real* earnings of a household over its life cycle.[4] Clearly, with some intertemporal borrowing and saving going on, it does not make sense to compare a flow of income during retirement to a particularly biased small subset of years prior to retirement.

Third, Social Security provides two types of extra insurance as compared with earnings. First and foremost, benefits are provided in the form of an annuity and hence may be valued at more than their expected present value if there are no actuarially fair private annuities available. With the date of death uncertain, households have to make the difficult choice between consuming their wealth too rapidly and therefore spending their very last years as paupers or consuming too slowly and leaving an unplanned bequest because of excess frugality late in life. The value of the Social Security annuity is therefore quite important. Second, Social Security benefits are a known amount and indexed against inflation. Earnings, in contrast, typically vary for lots of reasons—recessions, changes in tax rates, shifts in demand away from or toward the occupation of the head of household, etc. Risk-averse individuals will value the certainty of Social Security income more than an uncertain income flow with higher variance and identical mean. Just as there are "risk premia" for risky assets, a "certainty bonus" could be attached to Social Security benefits, independent of the extra premium, because of their annuity nature. That is, even if the date of death were known (say 10 years from retirement), obviating the need for annuities, the certain income from Social Security would be worth more than a fluctuating income whose mean value would equal the average Social Security payment.

Fourth, the elderly have very different types of expenses compared to those they had when they were younger. For example, they no longer have the expenses of rearing children—a large fraction of household budgets. But they may face substantial increases in other types of expenditures, such as for medical care. While most of their medical costs are paid for by Medicare, spending by the elderly on medical expenses has increased substantially. Further, extra medical expenditures should not necessarily be confused with a higher standard of living. It may be that income minus medical expenditures would be a better measure of well-being than gross income.

All of the above suggests that a series of adjustments should be made in the replacement rates in order to compare the command over resources after retirement to that prior to retirement.[5] Tables 2.5 through 2.7 present several of these types of corrections based on data from the Longitudinal Retirement History Survey.[6] They reveal that plausible adjustments for taxes, child expenses, risk, etc., are substantial. For example, using real career average earnings in the denominator (as opposed to using the 3 years of highest earnings during the 10 years prior to retirement) increases the Social Security replacement rate for married couples from 40 to 55 percent. It reaches *almost 100 percent* with tax, children, and certainty bonus adjustments. The adjusted Social Security replacement rate alone substantially exceeds "full" replacement for the poor elderly and is about four-fifths, two-thirds, and one-half for modest-, middle-, and upper-middle-income households. Only for wealthy elderly households (fewer than the

Table 2.5
Replacement Rates* Relative to Lifetime Indexed Average Earnings, 1979

	Social Security Benefits	Total Income
By Household Type:		
Married Couples	54.61%	101.61%
Widows	35.21	66.34
By Average Income Class:		
under $7,500	90.24	146.20
$7,500-12,499	54.50	92.37
$12,500-19,999	42.74	77.63
$20,000-29,999	32.12	66.72
$30,000-49,999	23.55	67.62
50,000+	10.89	57.31

* Based on author's calculations from Longitudinal Retirement History Survey. Data are price indexed, any year of retirement, career average income.

top 10 percent) does it dip below one half, and recall that these numbers do not include an annuity premium. Note also that the *total income* replacement rate often exceeds 100 percent by a substantial amount.

Thus, while the adjusted data do not necessarily mean that all of the elderly are better off than they were earlier in their life, they do cast considerable doubt on the proposition that Social Security is meager in its replacement; that the elderly are not very well-off relative to their earlier years; and that structural revisions in Social Security benefits will necessarily leave future generations of the elderly worse off in their retirement than they were in their working lives.

The importance of Social Security to the elderly is indicated in Table 2.8; Social Security benefits represent 37 percent of the

Table 2.6
Adjusted Replacement Rates* by Household Type, 1979

Household Type	Social Security Benefits	Total Income
Married Couples:		
Unadjusted	54.61%	101.61%
Adjusted for Taxes	60.53	110.68
Adjusted for Taxes and Children	77.85	142.51
Adjusted for Taxes, Children, & Risk	92.86	157.52
Widows:		
Unadjusted	35.21	66.34
Adjusted for Taxes	38.58	71.94
Adjusted for Taxes and Children	43.35	80.87
Adjusted for Taxes, Children, & Risk	52.37	89.71

* Based on author's calculations from Longitudinal Retirement History Survey. Data are price indexed, any year of retirement, career average income.

current total income of the elderly. Federal outlays on other retirement programs—Medicare, Medicaid, etc.—add substantially to this total, as shown in Table 2.9. Clearly, without Social Security, the average income of the elderly would decrease substantially, and a much larger fraction of the elderly would be destitute. Still, it should be kept in mind that the growth of Social Security benefits probably created a situation in which other forms of income support were reduced. For example, while the data are hardly definitive, they do seem to imply some reduction in private saving in anticipation of future Social Security benefits. Also, Social Security not only has replaced involuntary reduction in earnings due to involuntary retirement but has accelerated retirement decisions and supplanted continued earnings for a large fraction of the elderly, especially in the first few years after retirement. It is also clear that the substantial growth of Social

Table 2.7
Adjusted Replacement Rates* by Income Class, 1979

Income Class	Social Security Benefits	Total Income
under $7,500		
Unadjusted	90.24%	146.20%
Adjusted for Taxes	94.17	152.12
Adjusted for Taxes & Children	108.14	174.73
Adjusted for Taxes, Children, & Risk	140.55	206.18
$7,500-12,499		
Unadjusted	54.50	92.37
Adjusted for Taxes	58.89	98.39
Adjusted for Taxes & Children	69.65	116.45
Adjusted for Taxes, Children, & Risk	82.44	129.08
$12,500-19,999		
Unadjusted	42.74	77.63
Adjusted for Taxes	48.32	86.06
Adjusted for Taxes & Children	58.85	104.22
Adjusted for Taxes, Children, & Risk	66.20	111.59
$20,000-29,999		
Unadjusted	32.17	66.72
Adjusted for Taxes	37.95	76.39
Adjusted for Taxes and Children	47.49	95.48
Adjusted for Taxes, Children, & Risk	53.23	101.27
$30,000-49,999		
Unadjusted	23.55	67.62
Adjusted for Taxes	28.68	77.27
Adjusted for Taxes and Children	36.33	97.02
Adjusted for Taxes, Children, & Risk	43.99	104.24
$50,000+		
Unadjusted	10.89	57.31
Adjusted for Taxes	14.60	66.72
Adjusted for Taxes and Children	19.12	87.72
Adjusted for Taxes, Children, & Risk	26.20	95.15

* Based on author's calculations from Longitudinal Retirement History Survey. Data are price indexed, any year of retirement, career average income.

Table 2.8
Sources of Money Income for the Elderly,* 1981

Source	Percentage
Social Security	37
Earnings	25
Property Income	23
Pensions	13
Other	2

* Data is for elderly households. Persons living alone have a larger percentage of income from Social Security and a smaller percentage of income from earnings.

Source: U.S. Bureau of the Census, *Current Population Survey,* March 1982.

Security benefits has eased the pressure on younger workers to support their parents and grandparents with cash, living accommodations, and so on.

In summary, the data presented in Tables 2.4 through 2.7 should be interpreted as an upper bound on the extent to which Social Security contributes to the income of the elderly. For example, Table 2.5 suggests that, for married couples, the total income replacement relative to lifetime indexed average earnings in 1979 was about 100 percent. About half of this income replacement was due to Social Security benefits. Should it then be concluded that, in the absence of Social Security, the income replacement rate would be only one half? Surely if Social Security were removed overnight, this would be an accurate short-term prediction. But if the removal were gradual, any reduction in Social Security benefits (say, for wealthier retirees) could be accommodated by increased saving, additional earnings, or private, intergenerational, intrafamily income transfers. However, the substitution would be less than dollar for dollar, so we should conclude that Social Security, on average, has made a substantial contribution to the well-being of the elderly.

Table 2.9
Federal Government Outlays Benefiting the Elderly,
(Fiscal Year 1982)

Program	Percent of Total Spending Benefiting Elderly
Social Security	57
Medicare	22
Other Retirement	10
Medicaid	3
Housing	2
Veteran's Retirement	2
Supplemental Security Income	1
Other	3

Source: U.S. Bureau of the Census, Series P-23, No. 128, September 1983.

Three recent studies estimate the combined effect of Social Security benefits and taxes paid on net income or wealth position over the lifetime of households of different age, marital status, income levels, etc. These studies employ complementary techniques and data sources yet come to the same conclusion: there has been an *enormous* intergenerational redistribution of income toward current retirees from the general working population.

About four-fifths of the benefits of current retirees can be considered a transfer payment from the general population in the sense that cumulating their lifetime employer-employee taxes plus interest would provide only one fifth of the benefits they are receiving. Marcy Avrin, Kenneth Cone, and I estimate that this aggregate transfer across generations will amount to several trillion dollars over the next 75 years.[7] It will continue, for the average family, for approximately two decades, at which point the transfer will turn negative. Since at least part of the dramatic increase in benefits was unanticipated, it can be assumed that part of the reason the total income replacement rate often exceeds 100 percent is that the current generation of beneficiaries could not go back and spend some of this windfall earlier in their working lives. Michael Hurd and John Shoven reach a similar conclusion, as does Anthony Pellechio (see Table 2.10).[8]

Table 2.10
The Intergenerational Redistribution in Social Security

1. Windfall Gains and Losses for Families Reaching Age Sixty-Five in Various Years*

(in thousands of *discounted* constant value 1983 dollars)

Year Age Sixty-Five Is Reached	1977 or earlier	1982	1992	2002	2012	Thereafter
Average Tax Paid	10.5	27.5	51.0	80.0	110	—
Average Bene- fit Received	74.0	72.0	84.0	99.0	108	—
Average Net Benefit	63.5	45.0	33.0	19.0	-2.0	very large negative
Transfers as % of Total Benefit	86	63	39	19	-2.0	very large negative

Source: Updated from M. Boskin, M. Avrin, and K. Cone, "Modelling Alternative Solutions to the Long-Run Social Security Funding Crisis," in M. Feldstein, ed., *Behavioral Simulation Methods in Tax Policy Analysis* (Chicago: University of Chicago Press, 1983).

* Averages per family based on law in effect in 1982, under intermediate assumptions. The redistribution within age groups is discussed in Chapter 2.

Table **2.10** (*concluded*)

2. *Change in Present Value of Benefits Minus Taxes Due to 1983 Amendments if Carried Out*
($ 1983)

Type of Household	Age in 1983		
	25	40	55
One earner			
earnings=$15,000	-8,100	-7,100	-4,000
earnings=$35,700	-15,100	-11,200	-6,300
Two earners			
earnings=$15,000	-7,600	-6,100	-2,200
earnings=$35,700	-17,700	-11,000	-4,000

Source: Computed from A. Pellechio and G. Goodfellow, "Individual Gains and Losses From Social Security Before and After the 1983 Amendments," *Cato Journal,* Fall, 1983.

3. *Projected Internal Rates of Return by Age Cohort*

Earnings Profile	Year Household Head Reaches Sixty-Five				
	1970	1980	1995	2010	2025
Low	9.7	6.6	4.6	3.7	3.4
Medium	8.5	5.9	3.6	2.5	2.2
High	7.5	5.6	3.3	2.1	1.5

Author's calculations. Example for married couples in which only the husband works; assumes 1983 amendments are fully implemented.

These studies also demonstrate another important fact: while the replacement rates in Social Security are highest for the lowest income people, the transfers—in terms of absolute dollar amounts—are greatest for the nonpoor. That is, above and beyond replacing income for low-income retirees, Social Security is transferring billions annually from the general taxpaying working population to well-off retirees.

Thus, while the general perception of Social Security is that it is a program that primarily assists the elderly poor, in fact, Social Security benefits and transfers are substantial for middle-income households. Given sufficient notification prior to retirement, such households could easily alter their private saving and retirement decisions to accommodate a gradual decrease in Social Security benefit replacement rates without any substantial hardship. Hundreds of billions of dollars could be saved over the next few decades by reducing prospective future Social Security payments to the nonpoor. Getting rid of "welfare for the rich"—one of the major features of the model dual system I propose (described in detail in Chapter 8)—also would partially solve the equity, financial solvency, and adverse incentive effects of Social Security.

THE HEALTH OF THE ELDERLY

The numbers and percentages of the population over any specified age commonly considered elderly, say, 65 or 85, have grown substantially since the turn of the century. As Table 2.11 demonstrates, in 1900, only 4 percent of the population was 65 and over and only 0.2 of the population 85 and over. By 1980, these figures had increased to 11.3 percent and 1.0 percent, respectively. The reason for much of the growth of the older population in the first half of the century was the decline in death rates from accidents, parasitic diseases, and other nonchronic illnesses. The trend toward a continued aging of our society is expected to continue. (A similar trend is expected in most other advanced economies; in Japan, for example, it is expected to be even more dramatic.) The Census Bureau projects that the fraction of our population age 65 and over will double by the middle of the next century, and the fraction over the age of 85 will increase fivefold.

This rapid growth of the elderly population, which has significant implications for a wide number of economic, social, and political issues, will have a profound effect on Social Security and

Table 2.11
Growth of Older Population, Actual and Projected

Year	Percent of Population Sixty-Five and Over	Percent of Population Eighty-Five and Over
1900	4.0%	0.2%
1920	4.7	0.2
1940	6.8	0.3
1960	9.2	0.5
1980	11.3	1.0
1990	12.7	1.4
2000	13.1	1.9
2010	13.9	2.4
2020	17.3	2.5
2030	21.1	2.9
2040	21.6	4.2
2050	21.7	5.2

Source: U.S. Bureau of the Census, *Current Population Reports*, Series P-23, No. 128, September 1983

other retirement income support systems. To analyze the impact of this phenomenon, it is useful to turn to the aged support ratio—i.e., the number of aged persons per 100 working-age persons. This ratio, actual and projected, is presented in Table 2.12. As can be seen, it is relatively stable from 1980 until shortly after the turn of the century at about 20 per 100. But when the baby boom generation begins to retire early in the next century, the aged support ratio will rise precipitously, probably doubling from its current level by 2050.

This doubling is purely due to an increase in the number of older persons; the burden on the working-age population could be worse if health care costs rise relative to other costs.

The growth in the number of projected elderly persons and in the aged support ratio is not entirely due to the aging of the baby

Table 2.12
Aged Support Ratio,* Actual and Projected

Year	Ratio
1940	10.9
1960	16.8
1980	18.6
1990	20.7
2000	21.2
2025	33.3
2050	37.9

* Number of people aged sixty-five and over per one hundred people aged eighteen to sixty-four.

Source: U.S. Bureau of the Census, *Current Population Reports,* Series P-23, No. 128, September 1983.

boom generation. Concomitantly, since about 1965, there has been a substantial increase in the life expectancy of the elderly. Table 2.13 presents data on life expectancies at age 65 in various years. Currently, the life expectancy of 65-year-olds is a little over 14 years for men and 18 years for women. But the trustees of the Social Security Administration, in their *intermediate* forecast, predict that the life expectancy of males will increase by more than three years and that of females by more than four years by the time of the retirement of the baby boom generation. This expectation means not only that there will be a substantially larger fraction of older people, but also that, on average, they will be living longer. Thus, unless the typical ages of retirement drift upward considerably, the average length of the retirement period will continue to expand rapidly. There also will be more "old" old in the population, and the annuity value of Social Security retirement and hospital benefits will become much more important.

The pressure that these demographic trends will place on our public and private income-support systems is enormous.[9] It has been estimated that, in order to achieve a replacement rate of 100 percent of average lifetime earnings, the typical required saving

Table 2.13

1. Life Expectancy at Age Sixty-Five

Year of Sixty-Fifth Birthday	Years of Life Remaining	
	Male	Female
1940	11.9	13.4
1960	12.9	15.9
1980	14.0	18.3
1990	15.1	19.9
2000	15.7	20.8
2010	16.1	21.3
2020	16.4	21.7
2030	16.8	22.2
2040	17.2	22.6
2050	17.5	23.1

Source: Social Security Administration, Trustees Report, 1983.

2. Estimated Gain in Life Expectancy Due to Elimination of Major Diseases

Cancer	3 years
Cardiovascular-Renal Diseases	11 years

Source: U.S. Public Health Service, U.S. Life Tables by cause of death.
Substantial reduction in cancer would have only a modest impact on life expectancies. Progress against heart disease, however, would make quite conservative the estimates of future life expectancy gains.

rate during working years would be about 20 percent of earnings. This is the rate from which full replacement could be made from accumulated private saving with no Social Security. The corresponding saving rate for a replacement of 80 percent of earnings is approximately 15 percent. These estimates were made when life expectancies for the elderly were much lower and before the trend to earlier retirement and slower productivity growth. Thus, without Social Security, the required saving rate to provide what might be considered a reasonable replacement rate in old age is several times the typical saving rate (5 to 6 percent) in the United States.

These numbers are simply frightening. The private saving rate in the United States, which is low and falling, should be *rising* substantially to accommodate the longer life expectancies and greater number of elderly expected early in the next century. It is already far too low to provide anything like adequate saving, independent of Social Security, for the bulk of the population. But Social Security fills a large part of the void. The same study estimated that, given the nature of Social Security benefits at this time, the typical required saving rate would be cut in half.

In order to evaluate the overall capacity of our retirement systems to support the elderly, the question of their health must be addressed. To answer this question, various measures of health status can be used, ranging from evaluations by the elderly of their own health to quantitative statistics on death rates and other measures usually correlated with health.

Table 2.14 presents some of these interesting data. For example, it shows the substantial average annual decline in death rates from heart and cerebrovascular diseases and other causes from 1965 to 1980; inroads against heart disease were significant factors in the increase in life expectancy over this period. Only 8 percent of the elderly described their health as poor. While the number of days of restricted activity due to illness, on average, was about twice as numerous for the elderly as for the general population, of those elderly who were working, the average number of lost days at work due to illness was the same as for the general population. On the other hand, as people age, chronic conditions—ranging from arthritis to impairments of the back and spine to heart conditions—become prevalent. Fully 80 percent of the elderly reported at least one such chronic condition. Also, the elderly visit doctors about 20 percent more than the general population, utilize hospitals twice as frequently, stay twice as long, and spend twice as much on prescription drugs. Furthermore, each of these indicators increases for the very old, those 85 and over.

Overall, however, the elderly are in much better health now than they were in previous generations. The health status data presented above combined with recent and projected increases in

Table 2.14
Alternative Measures of Health

Average *annual* change in death
rates from all causes, 1965-80

	age:	65-74	−1.4%
		75-84	−1.0%
		85 and over	−2.1%

Described health as poor	8%
Major activity limited for health reasons	40%
Days of restricted activity due to illness, average, 1981, elderly vs. general population	40 vs. 19
Average number of lost work days due to illness, elderly vs. general	4.5 vs. 4.5
Percentage with at least one chronic condition	80%
Doctor visits of elderly as percentage of general population	120%
Frequency and length of hospitalization of elderly as percentage of general population	200%

Sources: National Center for Health Statistics, *Health, United States, 1982,* Dec. 1982, Table 9, and U.S. Bureau of the Census, *Current Population Reports,* Series P-23, No. 128, September 1983.

life expectancy buttress the case for an alternative definition of "elderly." My colleague, Victor Fuchs, proposes measuring length of time from death rather than length of time from birth.[10] His calculations suggest that, in 1983, a 72-year-old had the same 12.5-year life expectancy as a 65-year-old did in 1935. This statistic is startling when contemplated in light of the trend toward earlier retirement and the substantial increases in the projected number of elderly persons in the United States in decades to come.

While there will undoubtedly continue to be elderly who are disabled or who are severely limited because of poor health, it is an urgent priority to reevaluate the capacity of those over 65 to work beyond current typical retirement ages.

CONCLUSION

The data presented in this chapter on the absolute and relative economic well-being of the elderly, their health, their life expectancies, their Social Security replacement rates, and the intergenerational transfers made by Social Security, all suggest that the basic structure of Social Security benefits and taxes must be reconsidered. We are on a collision course with financial insolvency and a tremendous schism between generations. Even if this were not the case, there are compelling reasons for Social Security reform. Except in the case of the low-income elderly, future Social Security benefits will be larger than necessary, crowding out private saving, continued earnings, and private insurance. The Social Security system can be made much more cost-conscious and target-effective without impairing the well-being of future generations of elderly Americans.

CHAPTER **3**

Retirement Patterns and Policies

INTRODUCTION

Most of us think about retirement primarily in the context of our own careers and/or the situation facing friends and relatives. The general pattern of retirement in society, however, is important for many reasons. It affects the nature of the labor market, the well-being of the elderly, saving behavior, and public and private income-support programs for the elderly, such as Social Security and private pensions.

Consider the implications, for example, of the fact that the typical U.S. retirement age has gradually drifted downward from 65 to 62. Among other things, this implies a substantially longer retirement period, requiring increased private assets or public financial support. It also implies changes in the nature of communities housing the elderly and in intergenerational relations (one avenue of potential support for a longer retirement period). Early retirement patterns lead to a need for increased saving and may render the job mobility of those nearing retirement age more difficult (potential employers would not expect mature workers to remain on the job for any length of time).

Suppose the trend toward early retirement continues, or even accelerates, while at the same time we face the likelihood of increases in life expectancy, low saving rates relative to our own history and to the rest of the world, and a bulge of retirees when the baby boom generation retires early in the next century. While now there are over three workers for every retiree, most projections show this ratio declining to a point where, when the baby boomers retire, there will be fewer than two workers for each retiree. What this adds up to is a recipe for enormous economic, social, and political difficulty in everything from the financial solvency of the Social Security system to the adverse incentives of high taxes on subsequent generations to pay for the larger number and lengthier retirement period of the baby boomers who have saved so little.

Thus, it is important to examine retirement patterns and policies so that we can anticipate future problems and begin to develop sensible alternatives to the current, clearly unstable system. There have been tremendous changes in retirement patterns over time and an enormous diversity in retirement patterns among the current elderly. This information forms the foundation upon which any sensible changes in retirement policies must be based.

There are numerous definitions of retirement. Probably the

most common is leaving a career or job that has been held for a long period of time. While this definition certainly applies in a majority of cases, it is not uncommon for people to take on new jobs late in life—say, at age 60 or 65—and keep them for a few years. Nor is it likely that *all* of those employed at age 60 have been on the same job for a long period of time. Many of the elderly work part time, and there is substantial locational and job mobility among them. For example, in 1981, about half the working males and three fifths of the working females over the age of 65 were employed part time.[1]

Other definitions of retirement might well include no hours of work in the marketplace for a given period of time, say, a year; working far fewer hours than normal full time; or doing no work for pay (for example, housework or volunteer work). Whatever the merits or demerits of these various definitions, the important point is that retirement represents a substantial change in job-related activity characterized by a sharp, or continual and gradual, reduction in hours of work and probably in hourly wage rates as well.

RETIREMENT DECISIONS AND THE ECONOMY

Collectively, as well as individually, *each of us* has a substantial stake in the general pattern of retirement decisions in the United States because of the effects of those decisions on our economy. For example, if individuals decide to retire earlier, as has been the case in recent years, the average length of time between retirement and death will rise. And my own calculations suggest that each one-year increase in the length of the retirement period will increase the deficit in the Old-Age, Survivors, and Disability Insurance Program (OASDI) by approximately $.5 trillion.[2] This implies large tax increases to finance increased benefits in the future.

It is sometimes argued that the elderly's pattern of retirement has a significant impact on the general wage and employment structure in the economy. This argument, which is based on a "lump of labor" concept—that there are a fixed number of jobs and that, each time an individual retires, precisely one job is created—was one of the primary motivations for starting Social Security during the Great Depression. But in an economy such as ours, which tends toward close to full employment most of the time, this concept is false. In the United States, there is a complicated interaction of demand for different types of labor and supplies of labor with different skills, matched in a variety of interrelated markets and submarkets. A massive movement of the elderly out of the labor force at an earlier age, or an extended stay in the labor force beyond current expectations, could have some effect on the rates of promotion and the relative wage structure of workers of different experience; but these changes would not be large and continuous enough to cause a massive transformation in employment or unemployment. Rather, most economists believe that such changes can be absorbed gradually in our economy through modifications in relative wages and shifts in the location and type of job done by workers of different ages and skills. A telling example is the growth of employment—almost 30 million additional workers since 1970—due to the baby-boom generation and more married women entering the labor force without seriously affecting the opportunities for the elderly.

INCOME SUPPORT FOR THE ELDERLY

The level, extent, composition, and growth of public and private support programs for the elderly is a major concern, not only to the elderly themselves, but to the rest of the population as well—for these programs affect taxes paid by the general public and may influence the direct or indirect support provided to elderly parents, grandparents, other relatives, or friends. Consequently, the elderly's sources of income will be analyzed in a somewhat broader context than usual—i.e., in the context of an economy in which significant intergenerational and intrafamily transfers may occur, at least for a substantial number of individuals and families.

As can be seen from Table 3.1, the level of total income for the elderly varies markedly in the population. What is most striking, however, is the large number of retired elderly with low or moderate income. Over one half had a total income under $10,000 in 1980, while about one third had income in the $10,000 to $30,000 range, and only 7 percent had a total income of $30,000 or more. As discussed in Chapter 2, on average, these figures are roughly comparable to preretirement incomes. But continued earnings represent only a minor proportion—25 percent—of the income of the "young" elderly (see Table 2.8), and that figure is falling despite improved health and longer life ex-

Table 3.1
Distribution of Total Income in 1980, Households Headed by Those Sixty-Five Years Old & Over

Total Income	Percent of Elderly Households
Less than $5,000	25.9
$5,000-9,999	30.3
$10,000-19,999	26.8
$20,000-29,999	9.6
$30,000-50,000	5.3
$50,000+	2.0

Source: U.S. Bureau of the Census, *Current Population Reports,* Special Studies, Series P-23, No. 126, August 1983.

pectancies. While earned income has been replaced (primarily by Social Security benefits), problems may arise in providing larger benefits in the future. Thus it is natural to ask whether there is opportunity for somewhat greater reliance on earnings than at present.

Labor force participation rates for the elderly have been declining for some time. Table 3.2 documents the sharp drop in recent years of the labor force participation rates for elderly males. Shortly after World War II, half of the men over the age of 65 were in the labor force; today that number is under one fifth. More people now claim their first Social Security check at age 62 than at age 65. As a result of this trend toward earlier retirement, the elderly's share of income accruing from continued earnings has dropped substantially. If it is not replaced from other sources—including private and public pensions—the standard of living of the elderly will decline.

Retirement decisions and the economic well-being of the elderly have been influenced by changes that have occurred in our economy over the past few decades. The development of support systems for the aged—i.e., private pensions, Social Security, etc., to cover the bulk of the population—is a relatively recent phenomenon. Back when Social Security "targeted" the normal re-

Table 3.2
Labor Force Participation Rates for White Elderly Males,* Selected Years, 1948-82

	55-64 Years Old	65 Years Old & Over
1948	89.6%	46.5%
1953	87.7	41.3
1958	88.2	35.7
1963	86.6	28.4
1968	84.7	27.3
1973	79.0	22.8
1978	74.0	21.0
1982	70.7	17.6

* The pattern for nonwhite elderly males is quite similar.

Source: U.S. Bureau of Labor Statistics, *Special Labor Force Reports,* various issues.

tirement age as 65, our economy and society were quite different. Average incomes were much lower; there were far fewer families with two wage earners; the occupational, industrial, and locational structure of the labor force was substantially different; on average, families were much larger; there were far fewer single adults; a much smaller fraction of the population went on to higher education; and, perhaps most important, the life expectancy of the elderly was several years less than it is today. Changes in each of these areas has influenced not only the labor market conditions that affect retirement decisions, but also intrafamily and intergenerational exchanges of income and the interpretation of adequate income support during retirement. For example, because of the substantial increase in life expectancy, the same amount of assets adjusted for inflation at retirement would provide a smaller annual level of income for an elderly couple today than it would have two decades ago.

Although the well-being of the elderly depends to a considerable extent on conditions in the overall economy, intrafamily and intergenerational transfers of income also have a significant effect. In other societies, children are frequently expected to care for their elderly parents. Anecdotal information suggests that, several decades ago in the United States, a much larger fraction of elderly parents lived with their children and perhaps received some form of financial assistance from them. But the decline of family ties—in part due to the enormous locational mobility in the United States—and many other factors have combined to alter the nature of intrafamily transfers of income. The development of Social Security, unemployment insurance, and other government programs has *potentially* substituted not only for private accumulation of saving for retirement (and/or for periods of unemployment) but also for private intrafamily transfers of income.[3] In other words, Social Security benefits received by a family may not be assumed simply to add to total income; these benefits may partially replace continued earnings and affect the possibility of increased support from other family members or private saving. Thus the observed income of the elderly—in the aggregate and by source—at times *reflects decisions* made by the elderly and other family members about *when to retire*, patterns of intrafamily support, and lifetime saving patterns.[4]

RETIREMENT AND LABOR FORCE PARTICIPATION PATTERNS

The main question is whether the general decline in the labor force participation of elderly men in the United States will continue or whether it will reverse itself. In addition, will the growing number of working women adopt different retirement patterns than the smaller percentage of currently elderly women who had long work histories? Will they emulate current elderly men in their retirement behavior? Will future elderly men approaching retirement have work histories more similar to those of today's working women well below retirement age?

Tables 3.3, 3.4, and 3.5 reveal the labor force participation rates of elderly and near-elderly males and females, of females by marital status, and of blacks and other nonwhites compared to whites. While the bulk of the elderly labor force in the period under study is made up of white males, in the future, older fe-

Table 3.3
Labor Force Participation Rates by Age and Sex, Selected Years

	Male		Female	
Year	55-64 Years	65 & Over	55-64 Years	65 & Over
1960	85.2%	32.2%	36.7%	10.5%
1965	83.2	26.9	40.6	9.5
1970	81.5	25.8	42.5	9.2
1975	74.8	20.8	40.6	7.8
1978	72.5	19.7	41.1	7.8
1982	70.7	17.6	42.1	7.7

Source: U.S. Bureau of Labor Statistics, *Special Labor Force Reports.*

Table 3.4
Labor Force Participation Rates for Mature and Elderly Females, by Marital Status, Selected Years

	Married, Spouse Present		Single	
Year	45-64 Years	65 & Over	45-64 Years	65 & Over
1960	36.0%	6.7%	79.8%	24.3%
1965	39.5	6.7	76.1	22.4
1970	44.0	7.3	73.0	19.7
1975	43.8	7.0	68.3	15.8
1978	45.4	7.1	65.8	14.1
1982	47.8	7.1	64.8	13.0

Source: U.S. Bureau of Labor Statistics, *Special Labor Force Reports, Handbook of Labor Statistics.*

Table 3.5
Labor Force Participation Rates by Race, Sex, & Age, Selected Years

	Whites			
	Male		Female	
Year	55-64 Years	65 & Over	55-64 Years	65 & Over
1955	88.4%	39.5%	31.8%	10.5%
1960	87.2	33.3	36.2	10.6
1965	85.2	27.9	40.3	9.7
1970	83.3	26.7	42.6	9.5
1975	76.5	21.8	40.7	8.0
1977	74.7	20.2	40.8	8.0
1982	71.0	17.9	41.5	7.8

	Blacks and Other Nonwhites			
	Male		Female	
Year	55-64 Years	65 & Over	55-64 Years	65 & Over
1955	83.1%	40.0%	40.7%	12.1%
1960	82.5	31.2	47.3	12.8
1965	78.8	27.9	48.9	12.9
1970	79.2	27.4	47.1	12.2
1975	68.7	20.9	43.8	10.5
1977	67.0	19.3	42.7	9.9
1982	61.9	15.9	44.8	8.5

Source: U.S. Bureau of Labor Statistics, *Special Labor Force Reports, Handbook of Labor Statistics.*

males will be represented in greater numbers than they have been in the recent past. It is instructive to note (see Table 3.3) that the labor force participation rates of elderly females have actually declined slightly, although those for females approaching the years of normal retirement—i.e., in the age group of 55 to 64— have increased slightly since 1960.

Also, as presented in Table 3.4, marital status seems to have a significant effect on elderly females. For the past two decades, the labor force participation rate of married elderly females with a spouse present has been relatively stable at around 7 percent. For single elderly females, the labor force participation rates have declined somewhat but have remained substantially above those of married elderly females. A variety of factors—such as the increasing tendency toward two-earner families, greater instability in the longevity of marriages, and the greater increase in life expectancy for elderly females than for elderly males—all suggest that forecasting the labor force participation rates of elderly females and their responsiveness to public policies may be difficult.

Table 3.5 documents the decline in labor force participation of elderly nonwhite males; though similar to the trend for elderly white males, the falloff in participation for nonwhite males age 55 to 64 is less dramatic.

Table 3.6 lists a few of the reasons the elderly have given for not participating in the labor force for several selected recent years. Of particular importance is the relatively minor percentage of those 60 and over who list ill health as the primary reason for their nonparticipation. While it is undoubtedly true that, on average, health deteriorates late in life and some fraction of the elderly have serious impairments that prevent them from continuing to work either at their normal job or at any job, these data reveal that poor health is certainly not the overwhelming reason for the trend to earlier retirement and the decreased labor force participation of the elderly. Also, only a small (but growing) percentage report they are not in the labor force because they think they are unable to get a job or for other economic reasons. The overwhelming reason given by men for not participating in the labor force is that they are old and have decided to retire; elderly females overwhelmingly report home responsibilities as the reason for nonparticipation. While an assortment of interpretations could be drawn, the evidence from this survey suggests there is great variety as to the reasons different people retire at different ages and there is some degree of flexibility in their choice of retirement dates.

Table 3.6
Stated Reasons for Not Participating in the Labor Force by Persons Sixty & Over, Selected Years

Year	Ill Health	Home, School Responsi- bilities	Old Age/ Retire- ment	Economic Reasons	Other
Males					
1973	21.1	2.8	55.4	14.3	6.5
1977	15.6	2.3	56.3	17.6	8.2
1980	14.2	2.5	57.5	19.5	6.3
Females					
1973	18.0	12.3	38.4	18.5	12.9
1977	16.9	9.8	38.3	21.0	14.0
1980	13.3	9.9	40.4	23.8	12.6

Source: U.S. Bureau of Labor Statistics, *Special Labor Force Reports,* various years.

The decline in the labor force participation of the elderly did not occur in a vacuum. Dramatic and significant changes in the U.S. economy occurred simultaneously with the trend to earlier retirement and potentially affect, and are affected by, this trend. In addition, there is a long list of public and private policies that not only directly affect the desirability of work, but may also affect retirement through their interaction with saving and with insurance against ill-health, disability, and related contingencies. Among the most important of these policies are:

1. The level, growth, timing, and other features of Social Security and related public retirement benefits.
2. The auxiliary features of Social Security, such as survivors and hospital insurance.
3. Regulations, tax policies, and so on, affecting capital and insurance markets. Among these are the double taxation of some forms of saving under our income tax system and

the recent trend to allow the deductibility of certain types of saving (e.g., individual retirement accounts, employer prepaid pension and health programs, etc.).
4. Rules and regulations constraining the nature of pension programs and government insurance of such programs.
5. The growth of Medicare, unemployment insurance, and disability insurance coverage.

These policies can have important effects on retirement patterns. For example, if policies systematically make it more difficult for people to save for their own retirement, they will have to work longer and retire for a shorter period, *other things being equal.* On the other hand, public provision of retirement benefits plus various types of public insurance against the risks of disability and ill-health make it easier for people to retire at an earlier age, and free them of the need for continued earnings for insurance purposes.

HETEROGENEITY IN RETIREMENT DECISIONS

A potential source of the accelerated trend toward earlier retirement is the changing structure of employment. Table 3.7 details the enormous shift in civilian employment in the United States from agriculture to services. Whereas the proportion of civilians employed in industry has remained relatively stable over the past century, only about 1/15th as many civilians are engaged in agriculture today as compared with the period shortly after the Civil War; and only one quarter as many as in 1950, just three decades ago. At the same time, service employment has increased by one third since 1950.

Therefore, there is some plausibility to the conjecture that the rapid shift out of agriculture and into industries and services may be responsible for some share of the decline in the labor force participation of the elderly—at least until quite recently. But, as documented previously, the trend toward earlier retirement accelerated substantially around 1970, by which time only 4 percent of civilian employment was in agriculture. Thus, while the shift out of agriculture may have been a major reason for the decline in the labor force participation rate of the elderly from 1890 to the late 1940s, it has virtually nothing to do with the rapid reduction in the past decade or two—particularly for the group labeled "mature men" (those 55 to 64).

Table 3.7
Changing Structure of Civilian Employment in U.S. Economy, Selected Years

Year	Agriculture	Industry	Service
1870	47%	27%	26%
1900	35	34	32
1930	22	36	42
1950	12	42	46
1970	4	39	57
1978	3	36	60
1982	4	27	69

Source: Victor R. Fuchs, "Economic Growth and the Rise of Service Employment," *Towards an Explanation of Economic Growth,* ed. Herbert Giersch (Tubingen, West Germany: J.C.B. Mohr [Paul Siebeck], 1981); U.S. Bureau of Labor Statistics, *Handbook of Labor Statistics,* 1982.

Do today's workers differ in their retirement decisions across occupations and industries? In order to examine this question, retirement rates were calculated among elderly white males who had worked the previous year, by age and occupation (see Table 3.8) and by age and industry (see Table 3.9). In each table, for ease of exposition, only those aged 63, 64, and 65—ages of substantial retirement activity—are examined.

The calculations document substantial variation in retirement rates across occupations and industries at different ages. As seen in Table 3.8, at the earlier ages, retirement rates in some occupations are more than double those in others. For example, 63- and 64-year-old white male operatives have retirement rates more than double those of managers. At age 65, however, when full Social Security benefits become available, the retirement rates increase precipitously and converge to approximately 50 to 60 percent for virtually all occupational groups.

A similar calculation reveals marked variations in the propensity to retire according to industry group. It is clear from Table 3.9 that a group of industries with physically demanding and dangerous jobs—i.e., agriculture, mining, and manufacturing—

Table 3.8
Retirement Rates Among Elderly White Males Who Worked Previous Year by Age & Occupation

Age	Profes-sional/ Technical	Manager	Sales	Craftsman	Operative	Non-farm Labor
63	14%	9%	10%	20%	23%	20%
64	23	18	21	26	35	21
65	57	56	65	58	64	39

Source: Author's calculation from Longitudinal Retirement History Survey, 1969-77.

has retirement rates that are substantially higher than a set of industries with less onerous and risky types of labor—i.e., wholesale and retail trade, finance, and services. As expected, retirement rates rise with age within each industrial classification.

This evidence should make us wary of national retirement

Table 3.9
Retirement Rates Among Elderly White Males Who Worked Previous Year by Age & Industry

Age	Agriculture, Mining & Manufacturing	Wholesale/ Retail Trade, Finance, Service
63	23%	8%
64	32	13
65	65	40

Source: Author's calculation from Longitudinal Retirement History Survey, 1969-77.

policies that fail to allow substantial options for those who, for a variety of reasons, may wish to, or have to, retire at different ages.

There are two other significant issues related to the changing employment mix of the population and its likely impact on retirement probabilities. They concern the rapid increase in the number of people working for federal, state, or local governments and the corresponding growth in the level and coverage of non-Social Security retirement income programs for them. As of 1980, for example, the federal civil service retirement program had approximately 2.7 million active participants; the military retirement program had approximately 3.3 million. Approximately 10 million state and local government employees are covered by a hodgepodge of pension programs. These programs will be discussed in more detail below; my purpose here is to point out differences in retirement behavior among groups subject to different retirement programs.

Elizabeth Meier and Cynthia Dittmar discovered that, in 1978, for example, approximately 85 percent of military personnel receiving retirement pay were between the ages of 35 and 59, and 27 percent of the total were between the ages of 35 and 39.[5] Corresponding figures for those receiving nondisability pay are 93 percent and 29 percent. They found the average age of federal civil service annuitants receiving retirement benefits in 1978— under special provisions for occupations with hazardous duties— to be about 56 years. In the private sector as well as the state and local sectors, we see similar findings. For example, in Los Angeles in 1977, Meier and Dittmar found the average age of retirement to be 48 years for police and 53 for fire fighters; in New York State, the average age of retirement was 49 years for police. Certainly, some of these recipients just change jobs and become so-called double dippers, collecting two pensions. And as coverage and benefit levels under Social Security disability insurance have grown, the average age of recipients has drifted downward. In 1975, for example, almost half of disability benefits awarded went to disabled workers below the age of 55.

Thus, contributing to the early retirement trend (now inching toward age 62) is this subgroup of the population, many of whom are disabled or at least covered by disability benefits, that leaves the labor force before reaching normal retirement age. Two other important facts also must be kept in mind in examining the structure of retirement in our economy. One is the substantial increase in college enrollment in the post-World War II era, implying that a progressively larger fraction of workers has entered the labor force at a later age; the other is the considerable rise in the life expectancy of the elderly.

SOCIAL SECURITY AND THE DECISION TO RETIRE

Although retirement patterns have been shaped by structural changes in the U.S. economy, public and private policies also have influenced the elderly's desire for work. The most important of these policies is, of course, Social Security. Any analysis of its impact on the decision to retire must rest on a reasonable treatment of a very complex set of laws and expectations. The factors most critical to an understanding of the recent trend toward early retirement are the nature of benefits calculation, the earnings test, and the changes in benefit levels mandated by Congress from 1968 to 1974.

Social Security benefits are a complicated function of previous Social Security contributions. For example, if a worker works an extra year rather than retiring at, say, age 62, he is allowed to replace a year of zero or low earnings in the calculation of his average monthly earnings with a year of greater earnings. This has the effect of raising his Social Security benefits, but the increase will vary from worker to worker because of differences in earnings histories. Some researchers suggest that the magnitude of this delayed retirement effect is substantial and negates any loss of benefits for additional work for those retiring before age 65. In fact, in a recent study, Michael Hurd and I conclude that the lost benefits for those working another year before age 65 (down to 62) were approximately offset by the increased benefits due to recalculation based on another year's earnings.[6]

Retirement after age 65, however, is another story. Future benefits are increased by the delayed retirement credit but at a much lower rate than such benefits are likely to be discounted by the elderly. The Social Security system, therefore, offers strong incentives to retire at age 65.

In addition, the Social Security system has an earnings test that reduces benefits 50 cents per dollar for earnings beyond a modest amount in the years prior to age 70. Again, this earnings test bites hardest after age 65; because of the recalculation of benefits between age 62 and 65, it has a lesser impact then.

Social Security affects retirement benefits in two major ways.

First, consider the case where a reduction in benefits does not cause any net transfers among individuals of different age/marital status/income levels. Under these assumptions, the system should not have any effect before the age of 65: each individual has the same lifetime resources regardless of retirement age and so will want to consume the same amount of "leisure," including retirement years. Furthermore, the age of retirement can be chosen independently of the age at which benefits can be drawn, *provided* the individual has sufficient private assets that can be consumed before eligibility for Social Security benefits.

If the foregoing is true, why would anyone retire at age 62? Retirement at age 62 will tend to occur if, in response to Social Security benefits, some people choose not to accumulate much private saving. Suppose Social Security taxes are so high that some workers find they accumulate more in Social Security benefits the total saving they desire. Their response to this high "forced saving" is to reduce their private saving to zero, and, if there were a capital market in which they could borrow against future Social Security benefits, they would retire at the age dictated by their lifetime wealth. If that age were earlier than the age of initial eligibility under Social Security, their consumption until that age would be financed by borrowing.

However, such capital markets do not exist. People *must retire* to draw on their Social Security benefits. Because the consumption of Social Security benefits is tied to the consumption of leisure, the Social Security system will have an effect on retirement for those people who have been forced to oversave. Michael Hurd and I found that people who have a high level of Social Security benefits relative to their other wealth will not retire before age 62.[7] They will have a disproportionate propensity to retire at age 62, compared to people with the same total wealth and a higher fraction of private wealth. I have labeled this relationship of Social Security to total wealth the *liquidity constraint* effect and discovered substantial impacts on retirement at age 62. Indeed, conditional retirement probabilities more than double between age 61 and 62, then decline to age 63. They triple between ages 64 and 65, then drop rapidly at age 66 and thereafter.

One of the most significant ways in which Social Security affects retirement is by a dramatic, especially unexpected change in the level of benefits. The sharp increases authorized by Congress in the late 1960s and early 1970s were unanticipated and not only enhanced the wealth of the elderly but (assuming "leisure" behaves in a normal manner) caused a speed-up in retirement. Had people been able to foresee the gigantic increases in Social Security benefits, they might have consumed more earlier in their life—including more leisure. But they were unable to go back and redo their previous consumption and leisure profile, so their retirement patterns accelerated. Again, Hurd and I found that the acceleration in the decline of the labor force participation of the elderly from 1969 to 1973 was *primarily* due to the large increase in real Social Security benefits.[8] Other researchers have come to similar conclusions, although the evaluation of the magnitude of the effect varies among different studies.[9]

IMPLICATIONS OF THE CHANGING AGE STRUCTURE OF OUR POPULATION

A further word needs to be said about the changing age structure of the population, because it potentially affects not only retirement decisions but also future Social Security taxes, the viability of the private pension system, and the long-term relationships among overlapping generations in our society.

What does the enormous impending change in the proportion of the elderly and the young in our population imply? Among the more significant implications are the following:

1. Financial pressures on Social Security.
2. Rapidly changing demand for different types of products.
3. Changing levels of experience among workers in the labor force and, hence, probably relative wages of workers of different ages.
4. The possibility of major changes in financial markets due to the pressure of a much larger percentage of assets being held by those drawing down rather than building up their assets.
5. Substantial pressure to alter immigration policy to reduce the strain on Social Security taxpayers.
6. A reevaluation of public spending as well as private spending programs—i.e., public education—on youthful dependents and therefore a potential dramatic change in intergovernmental fiscal relations.
7. Dramatic changes in the economic incentives and pressures for private intergenerational, intrafamily transfers of income.

This list, while not exhaustive, suggests that continuing policies and programs encouraging early retirement will place severe strains on our economy and society.

The changing age structure of the population also puts the private pension system under considerable potential strain. Many private pensions are not fully funded and, hence, face problems analogous to those of Social Security in financing future benefits to large groups of retirees. The same is true of many state, local, and federal pension programs. These problems not only interact with those of the Social Security system but often add considerably to the overall difficulties of providing long-term, secure retirement income.

Thus, just as the baby boom generation caused dramatic changes in earlier stages of its life cycle—such as the rapid expansion of expenditures on education in the 1950s and 1960s—so it will dramatically change labor markets and the demand for different types of products as it works its way through the labor force. At stake are the current and future retirement income of the elderly and their means of support. Indeed, the changing age structure of our population continues to affect virtually all aspects of current and future retirement decisions and the policies that influence them.

To summarize briefly, the trend to earlier retirement has been affected by a substantial number of major changes in the overall performance (and expected future performance) of our economy, as well as by a variety of public policies and private programs. The desire to retire early may well have resulted from a number of factors, including general real income growth, which in turn may have helped generate a variety of the institutions— such as public and private pension programs, mandatory retirement rules, housing programs, etc.—that affect the retired and potentially retired population.

THE NEED FOR COORDINATED POLICIES

The complicated interaction of policies affecting retirement and, perhaps more importantly, the enormous heterogeneity among current and prospective elderly individuals and households make it very difficult to fashion a single, overall system.

The growth of Social Security taxes and benefits certainly changes the relative attractiveness of, and dependence on, private pensions. Many firms are moving to integrate private pensions with Social Security by setting an overall contribution level for the two systems. Additional programs—relating to health insurance, the tax treatment of savings, regulation of private pensions, and antidiscrimination in the labor market with respect to the continued employment of the elderly—and a variety of other policies commingle to form a milieu in which incentives are generated or obstructed in the process of saving for one's own retirement. Thus, the future economic well-being of the elderly—and of the taxpayers—depends on a complicated system of interrelated policies and the actions or reactions induced by it. Against the backdrop of the population's rapidly changing age structure and the enormous long-term financial problems this implies for Social Security and other public and private retirement programs, there is ample scope for improving coordination among these policies, developing new policies, and altering existing ones to improve the efficiency and equity of not only the income support of the elderly, but also the overall functioning of our economy.

Finally, the desirability of neutrality in most economic decisions—such as the choice between saving and spending, or working and retiring—must be reiterated. The interaction of policies affecting such decisions has caused severe distortions in these choices.

SOME VEXING QUESTIONS

We are faced with a tough dilemma. Since a variety of public and private programs either induce, or at least coexist with, a trend to early and even very early retirement, we may see not only a large increase in the ratio of retirees to workers early in the next century, but *a still more dramatic change in the ratio of aggregate retirement years to aggregate working years* in the general population over time. Is this development socially desirable? Are the interrelated, but usually uncoordinated, public and private policies really *neutral* with respect to retirement decisions? Or are they a response to pressure for voluntary earlier retirement from our aging workers? Have these policies failed to keep up with rapidly changing economic, demographic, and labor market conditions, and do they therefore threaten both the income security of future elderly retirees and the taxpaying capacity of the general population? In a nutshell, are the variety of policies affecting retirement a natural evolution in response to market and political forces, or are they, at least partially, outmoded and anachronistic?

First, excluding the few exceptions to be noted, systematic distortions of incentives are undesirable, and therefore policies that potentially affect retirement should be designed to be as *neutral* as possible. Unfortunately, a variety of current policies—including Social Security benefits, the tax structure, historically relevant mandatory retirement rules, and various other policies—have systematically biased the decision toward earlier retirement. Such policies misallocate resources in the sense that a higher level of economic well-being could be attained if the distortions were removed and a neutral program put into place.

The exception occurs when it can be determined decisively that third parties are affected by the retirement decisions of the elderly. The implied reduction in living standard presumably might make those individuals with close ties to the elderly potentially worse off. Consequently, the individuals affected may voluntarily, if begrudgingly, adopt arrangements to support the elderly. It is important to remember that the benchmark ought to be neutrality and that the burden of proof for external benefits and/or costs should be placed on those proposing policies that distort the choices.

Thus, in a free market, it is desirable not to distort choices but rather to fashion public policies with respect to retirement income benefits to be *age neutral*. However, many problems—such as imperfect labor and capital markets—interfere with this ideal first-best world.

For example, where there are many job opportunities and many potential workers to fill them, it might be expected that competition in the labor market would efficiently match employees with jobs. The limitations of the elderly—such as their possibly shorter job tenure, their difficulties with mobility, insurability, etc.—which might affect the demand for their labor and employers' decisions whether to hire aging workers, *could* be compensated for by lower wages. But the demand for part-time labor may be insufficient to provide the desired level of employment for aging workers. Therefore, they may be faced with second-best choices—e.g., working full time or not at all, or not for pay in a volunteer job, or living in a location that is less than desirable.

Also, while it might be expected that the supply and demand for labor would equilibrate at a wage-plus-fringe-benefits level equal to the marginal product of labor, it may be difficult for a firm that has a group of aging workers who have been together for some time to adjust wage rates. If the current wage rate reflects the current rate of productivity, the older workers, because of their lower productivity, would suffer much larger wage declines compared to their peers. Indeed, the difficulties of reducing wages when productivity drops late in life—due to physical problems or obsolescence of technological knowledge and skills— may be a major reason why mandatory retirement policies were adopted in the first place.

In any event, despite the imperfect, real world, *some* bunching of leisure late in life is to be expected. An average decline in daily work of a quarter or half an hour does not leave much time to play golf or see the grandchildren, whereas an extra year or 2 of retirement may open up more possibilities for the enjoyment of leisure. Furthermore, as people become wealthier (real per capita income approximately doubled in the United States from 1948 to 1970), they consume more of all goods and services, including leisure, with this bunching effect at retirement. All other things being equal, therefore, a trend to early retirement should be anticipated.

In addition, there is something of a snowball effect in retirement decisions. As more and more of one's peers retire, it becomes more acceptable to do so. Also, the cost of being retired declines as a larger and larger concentration of elderly individuals lowers various costs in providing services.

Thus, some decrease in the labor force participation of elderly workers should have been expected anyway—purely due to an increase in wealth—even if there had been no gain in life expectancy, no shift out of physically demanding and dangerous jobs, and no late labor force entry. But these other changes could also work strongly in the opposite direction—i.e., they might increase the desire for work. Clearly, the trend to earlier retirement has been abetted by the enormous growth of transfer payments to the elderly under Social Security and the provision of a variety of government insurance programs such as those for hospitalization and disability.

To illustrate the factors instrumental in determining retirement, consider the simplest possible situation in which the date of death is known with certainty, there are no capital markets of any kind, and no health or disability problems exist. Since there are no capital markets, people consume what they earn. Knowing

Figure 3.1
Stylized Retirement, and Wealth Patterns with Alternative Assumptions

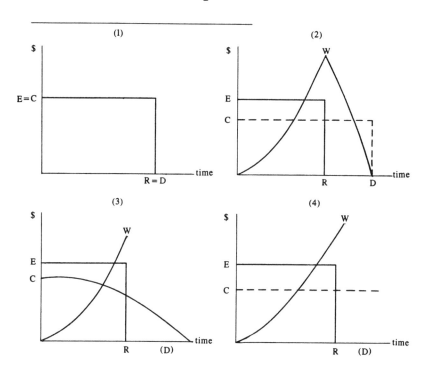

E=earnings (assumed constant for convenience)
C=consumption (with time preference=interest rate will be constant in (1), (2) and (4), but will decline in (3) due to extra discounting by mortality probabilities)
W=accumulated wealth (assets)
R=retirement date
D=known date of death
D ( )=uncertain date of death

their date of death and the fact that they have no health or disability problems, people will work to the day they die, with their consumption equaling their earnings. As a result, retirement is determined biologically (see Figure 3.1, panel 1).

Now let there be capital markets, however imperfect. This possibility is displayed pictorially in the second panel of Figure 3.1. Again, with no health or disability problems and a certain date of death, retirement will now be determined by the preferences for leisure versus work and the wage opportunities of the worker. Typically, retirement—financed by savings—will occur before the date of death.

If there is uncertainty about the date of death, one can never be sure that the accumulated savings generated during working years will be sufficient to finance consumption during retirement. Consequently, a difficult choice must be made between consuming too rapidly and thus running the risk of living "too long" and becoming a pauper late in life, and consuming too slowly and leaving an unplanned bequest (see panel (3)). Only with actuarially fair annuities markets will this type of problem be eliminated, as in panel 4 of Figure 3.1 (where wealth is used to purchase an annuity).

Thus, while quite simple in their assumptions, the examples given reinforce the potential avenues through which policies affect retirement decisions—e.g., lifetime resources, the distribution of those resources when capital and labor markets are imperfect, the nature of capital and insurance markets when dealing with risks and savings, etc.

CONCLUSION

Winston Churchill characterized Russia as a "mystery inside a puzzle wrapped up in an enigma." It is tempting to paraphrase Churchill in describing the problems plaguing our Social Security system, the difficulties surrounding recent retirement patterns of the elderly, and efforts made to determine their economic well-being. The rapid growth of Social Security benefits and coverage has enabled us to virtually eliminate poverty among the elderly and just about guarantee standards of living for the elderly no lower than those they had earlier in their working lives. But Social Security faces long-term financial insolvency. A major cause of the problem is that there will be *too many retired person years relative to working person years* beginning early in the next century. Part of this equation simply relates to how long people work prior to retirement.

The reasons for adopting and expanding policies that encourage people to retire earlier than they normally would are no longer valid in light of improved employment relative to the Depression, demographic changes, and the long-term financial solvency problems of social programs. Certainly, it is desirable to guarantee that those legitimately disabled or otherwise unable to work have an adequate safety net prior to an advanced retirement age. But it is clear that thinking of 65 as an age at which people are "worn out, washed up, or over the hill" no longer accords with their health status and economic potential.

Because Social Security has been sold as an analogue to an insurance system—even if it is financed on a pay-as-you-go basis—the huge transfers to well-off elderly people, which are scheduled to continue for three decades or more at the expense of the general taxpaying population, are hidden from view. This "welfare for the rich" is simply inexcusable.

Fuel is added to the fire by our low saving rate and the potential displacement of various types of private insurance programs, explicit and implicit, by the growth of Social Security beyond its basic and legitimate functions.

The shift out of dangerous and physically demanding jobs, later labor force entry due to college enrollment, the great increases in life expectancy, and the enormous potential for continued work by the elderly suggest two structural revisions in Social Security, upon which rest not only the solutions to its problems, but also the stability and effectiveness of the retirement income of future generations of American citizens. First, the structure of benefits should be tied much more closely to contributions; this would reduce excess returns to well-off individuals. But we should maintain ample benefits for those who must, for health reasons, retire early or have low levels of contributions and little other income. Second, there should be substantial increases (gradually phased in) in the age of eligibility for full retirement benefits. If this is done, private saving, private pensions, private insurance agreements, and labor market conditions for the elderly can all adjust to the elimination of public policies that induce people to retire earlier than they would like.

CHAPTER 4

Evaluating Social Insurance Options

INTRODUCTION

In order to accumulate assets out of which to finance retirement or to provide insurance against untoward contingencies, most working Americans must save—i.e., they must spend less than they earn. If there were no risks of ill health or disability or unemployment that could affect an individual's earnings stream, then putting aside a certain fraction of income over a given number of years (assuming compound interest) would allow for retirement with an assured amount of accumulated assets to finance future consumption. But these risks loom large. Indeed, one of the major motives for saving is precaution.

Increasingly, however, private firms are offering their workers pensions and prepaid health and related insurance programs. The private pensions come in various forms but are basically an attempt to provide old-age annuities. The health insurance programs primarily insure against various types of health care costs incurred prior to age 65.

A variety of difficulties, however, impinge on the private sector when it seeks to provide disability and health insurance and retirement annuities which are actuarially fair (i.e., at costs based on the true probabilities). These relate to the problems of adverse selection and moral hazard.

Adverse selection of risk is a situation where the "bad-risk" individual opts for insurance and the "good-risk" individual systematically avoids insurance. Adverse selection occurs, for example, when a health insurance company is not fully informed about an individual's proclivity to contract disease. Since those in the population who think their health risks are above average are more likely to sign up for a health insurance program than those who think their health risks are below average, there will be an adverse selection of risks in favor of the most risky, and the private insurance company involved could find itself going broke if the worse-than-average outcomes occurred. To protect against this possibility, the only way the insurance can be sold is at rates *above* those that would be actuarially fair for the entire group. Consequently, there are limits on the ability of private insurance to provide complete actuarially fair protection. If adverse selection were severe, the companies would go broke. Still, private insurance seems to do a reasonably effective job in the area of medical care, although the problem of adverse selection becomes most severe in cases of substantial impairments that require particularly expensive medical services. Suffice it to say that, for cata-strophic illnesses and disabilities, private insurance is likely to be more expensive than actuarially fair insurance. The only way around this problem is to form one large group and require com-pulsory coverage so there is no systematic opting in or out based on better information than that available to the insurer.

The problem of adverse selection may be exacerbated by the difficulty of accounting for moral hazard. Simply put, some risks can be increased or decreased by the behavior of the insured. (For example, those with theft insurance can alter the probability of burglary by using alarms.) This stumbling block occurs because, under a variety of insurance types and contractual arrangements, insured individuals have opportunities to adjust their behavior so as to increase the probabilities of risk. Moral hazard is a particular problem when the behavior of the insured is not easily monitored by the parties on the other side of the contract—i.e., insurance companies. Consider the case of disability insurance. An individ-ual might engage in activities that substantially decrease—or avoid activities that substantially increase—the probability of dis-abilities. He could refrain from driving while intoxicated or en-gaging in dangerous activities. But the extent to which an individ-ual does so is not easily monitored, except at extreme cost, by the potential insurer.

Consequently, the problems of adverse selection and moral hazard suggest that private insurance markets will not always work according to simple, classic textbook models of supply and demand, perfectly balancing the marginal value of additional in-surance with the incremental costs of providing it.

Partly for these reasons and partly for political, social, and other considerations, most social insurance programs provide the five basic interrelated types of coverage offered by Social Secu-rity: (1) retirement benefits in the form of annuities; (2) disability benefits in the form of annuities; (3) spousal survivors benefits; (4) dependent children survivors benefits; (5) hospital insurance. The efficiency, equity, and financial feasibility of any one of these can be evaluated only in terms of the entire package.

Decisions concerning retirement, saving, and insurance are made simultaneously, and each is potentially influenced by, and in turn influences, Social Security benefits. For example, retire-ment affects resources by decreasing earnings; it may also de-crease related benefits. But clearly the resources potentially avail-able to an individual in retirement are one of the considerations used in making the retirement decision itself. Likewise, certain health impediments will encourage early retirement, but retirement itself has the potential to affect physical and psychological health. Given that health care and disability expenditures are a substantial fraction of outlays for many elderly people, how can the adequacy of retirement income be determined if the adequacy of provision for health care and disability in old age is not known? Thus, any policy that affects Social Security coverage in any one area is likely to have effects on related programs. Increasingly, the age at which an individual becomes eligible for retirement benefits may affect private savings, earnings, and the propensity to apply for disability benefits.[1] Thus, an evaluation of the efficiency, equity, and continued financial feasibility of the Social Security system must be made against the backdrop of private intrafamily, intergenerational transfers of income, the possibility of continued earnings, and the opportunity for private saving and insurance arrangements.

SOCIAL SECURITY AND EFFICIENCY

In order to evaluate public policy on retirement, the efficiency of Social Security will be judged according to three basic standards. The first measure of efficiency, which is generally considered the most important by economists, calls for an attempt to balance the incremental value of society's resources with its opportunity cost—i.e., its value shifted to another use. This measure of efficiency tries to keep distortions of major economic decisions—such as labor supply, retirement, saving, and the purchase of various types of insurance—to a minimum. The level and nature of benefits, as well as their means of finance, can have very different effects on these types of decisions. People should not be told when to retire; nor should they be forced to purchase various types of insurance or to save if they have full information and if competitive markets exist for the provision of these services. Unless there were thought to be some major deviation between social and private valuations in these decisions (perhaps due to the involvement of third parties), keeping these distortions to a minimum is extremely important.

A second measure of efficiency relates to general administration. What fraction of resources is used directly to administer the Social Security program? What additional private resources are necessary to deal with it? Certainly, it would substantially underestimate the administrative cost of Social Security to look only at the expenditures of running the Social Security Administration. Beneficiaries and potential beneficiaries, as well as taxpayers, have a large number of time-consuming and costly obligations to fulfill. For example, many persons approaching the usual retirement age are uncertain of the level and the nature of the coverage they will receive under Social Security. Obtaining that information, given the enormous complexity of the Social Security benefit formula, is not always easy. While branch offices assist people attempting to obtain this information, they are severely restricted in their ability to provide it. Thus, because of the difficulty in ascertaining the level of Social Security coverage, the Social Security system may impose substantial uncertainty and administrative costs in planning for private insurance.

The third measure of efficiency is the target effectiveness of a program. Of the resources extracted from the private sector to finance a program publicly, what fraction goes to serve the goals of the program and what fraction goes to serve other persons, institutions, or groups? For example, the goal of the program may be to prevent destitution by guaranteeing an income to a particular group—e.g., the elderly—in order to keep it above the poverty line. In so doing, however, it may also transfer substantial resources to the nonpoor. Or the program may fall short of the mark and not eliminate poverty entirely among the elderly. The target effectiveness of a program is an important ingredient in the evaluation of public policy. Of course, the target effectiveness of Social Security expenditures is heavily influenced by the extent to which it alters retirement and saving decisions.

ECONOMIC EFFICIENCY: IMPACT ON THE LABOR MARKET

Social Security has been a major reason for the sharp decline in the labor force participation of the elderly and for the trend toward earlier retirement. Depending on one's point of view, this could be a blessing, a curse, or neither. An important question is whether, other things being equal, Social Security is inducing people to retire before they would like to. If true, the Social Security system would be distorting labor markets and contributing to an inefficient allocation of resources.

There are several ways in which Social Security may be inducing people to retire before they so desire. The most significant of these is the delayed retirement credit, which increases benefits for persons retiring after age 65 at a much lower rate than the elderly discount those benefits. While the 1983 amendments raised the credit, it is still actuarially unfair. Therefore, the present value of Social Security benefits is maximized for most families at age 65 and, not surprisingly, there is a big peak in the retirement probability at that age. If the delayed retirement credit were made actuarially fair—i.e., if beyond a certain age the present value of the benefits were independent of the age of retirement—people would not be induced to retire earlier than they otherwise would like.

Another way by which Social Security may be distorting the labor market is related to the earnings test. For many receiving Social Security, benefits are reduced 50 cents for each dollar of earnings, thus acting like a 50 percent tax. The earnings test increases the probabilities of retirement for those who would like to work, at least part time, when elderly. While the earnings test has been liberalized—both with respect to exempt amounts and the time span to which it applies—gradually eliminating it makes sense.

ECONOMIC EFFICIENCY: IMPACT ON PRIVATE SAVING

Social Security also potentially affects private saving. The anticipation of Social Security benefits at retirement may reduce incentives for private saving to provide for disemployment and contingencies. And less private saving may cause economic growth to suffer. Recall that Social Security is an unfunded, pay-as-you-go system; therefore, no real capital accumulation occurs when taxes are paid into Social Security because the money is immediately disbursed as benefits to current retirees.

Several researchers, most notably Martin Feldstein and Alicia Munnell, argue that Social Security depresses private saving.[2] Feldstein, argues that Social Security has two potentially offsetting effects. First, it induces people to retire earlier than they otherwise would; since this increases the length of the retirement period, it should lead, other things being equal, to an increase in planned saving for retirement. Second, Social Security is perceived as a source of wealth; consumers substitute this wealth for ordinary saving for retirement, therefore decreasing aggregate private saving. Feldstein's original empirical study, published in 1974, implied that the effect of the growth of Social Security was to reduce private saving almost dollar for dollar. Since private saving results in real capital formation and Social Security does not, Feldstein concluded that the growth of Social Security in the United States sharply curtailed capital formation, productivity, and national income.

Since the 1974 Feldstein and Munnell papers, there have been a variety of others both supporting and criticizing the analytical apparatus and the empirical estimates presented. The most important of these papers is the 1974 critique by University of Rochester economist Robert Barro.[3] His analysis diametrically opposes Feldstein's empirical results: Social Security's direct effect on private saving is exactly offset by private intrafamily, intergenerational adjustments, and hence Social Security has no impact whatsoever on aggregate private saving.

In Barro's analytical paper, a model of overlapping generations is developed whereby the well-being of a representative individual in each generation depends not only on his own lifetime consumption but also on the *utility* of his heirs; thus, *all* generations are linked. This linkage occurs because parents are concerned about the well-being of their children, but their children's well-being depends on the well-being of their children, and so on. In such a model, the fact that substantial positive bequests currently pass from the older to the younger generation in the United States has striking implications for the interpretation of Social Security's potential effects on private saving. Barro notes that these positive bequests imply that the current generation *already* has the opportunity to adjust its legacy to future generations by altering the level of private intergenerational transfers. The introduction of Social Security increases the wealth of the current generation but creates a corresponding liability for future generations. The current generation could resist the intergenerational redistribution of wealth by choosing not to allow these resources to be transferred to themselves, e.g., by increasing their bequests. The current generation would just increase their bequest by an amount sufficient so that their heirs are no worse off than before the introduction, or growth, of the Social Security system. The extra saving for this bequest just offsets the decreased saving due to Social Security.

While there is undoubtedly a substantial kernel of truth in Barro's argument, there are a variety of issues that his analysis ignores and a paucity of data on private intrafamily, intergenerational bequests.[4] For example, although total bequests are clearly positive, only a small number of people leave even modest direct gifts to their heirs.[5] Indeed, in light of the real income growth between generations, Feldstein has argued that many would like to leave negative bequests, which are not enforceable.[6] Even considering Social Security, the optimum may be zero inheritance for many families.

Of course, there is still much debate about how child-rearing and educational expenditures should be treated within the intergenerational bequest framework. Are such expenditures really *inter vivos* gifts? Would they have been made anyway? Are they consumption or investment? Should the large growth in public spending on higher education, which roughly coincided with the huge growth in Social Security, be considered an offset to Social Security? Since there is insufficient empirical data on such questions and since the data that exist are unreliable and difficult to interpret, people have drawn diametrically opposite conclusions.[7] It is clear, however, that "bequests" of human capital have a very different nature from bequests of ordinary capital: their liquidity, risk, and tax situations, and their ability to be transferred, are not the same.

A further issue deserves mention: the possibility of a distinction between the willingness to bequeath on a collective basis and the willingness to do so on a private basis. This conjecture has been made in other contexts by Amartya Sen and Steven Marglin.[8] It may well be that, given the nature of private capital markets, changing family relationships, and a variety of other factors, Social Security and private bequests are not perfect offsets to one another. Further, due to real income growth, it may well be that younger, wealthier generations would be willing to transfer greater resources to older, poorer generations on a collective basis—as a public good—than they would, when summed individually, bequeath privately.

Thus, a variety of considerations render the stylized models of Feldstein and Barro merely a place to start in attempting to evaluate the impact of Social Security on private saving and, *ipso facto,* capital investment and economic growth. The ultimate resolution of this important issue is an empirical question.

EMPIRICAL RESEARCH ON SOCIAL SECURITY AND SAVING

In the past decade, numerous empirical studies have tested the conflicting analytical conjectures about the effects of Social Security on private saving. Again, the seminal piece of research on this issue is that of Feldstein.[9] In his paper, Feldstein estimates consumer expenditures by relating them to the standard variables—such as disposable income, wealth, and retained earnings—that economists use. His novel contribution is to introduce, and propose a way to measure, the concept of Social Security wealth. Social Security wealth is an attempt to use the present value of expected future Social Security benefits to which the working population is "entitled" as a measure of the magnitude of the Social Security program's potential effects on private saving.

Social Security benefits and taxes can be thought of in a variety of ways by individuals making consumption/saving choices. For example, an individual can look at expected future retirement benefits, in present value terms, as an asset in his retirement income portfolio, while looking on taxes paid in the future as reductions in future disposable income. This is the concept that Feldstein proposes most often and labels "gross" Social Security wealth. On the other hand, an individual might subtract the present value of expected future taxes from the present value of expected future benefits to arrive at the net addition of the entire Social Security program to his "perceived wealth." This is usually labeled "net" Social Security wealth. Another possibility is to look at accumulated Social Security taxes and to measure the Social Security program's effect, treating it implicitly as a defined contribution plan.

Feldstein analyzed U.S. aggregate time series data for the period 1929 to 1971, excluding the war years. Using a variety of definitions and sample periods, he found that for each $1 increase in Social Security wealth, private saving decreased by $1. Since gross Social Security wealth is enormous, running to trillions of dollars, Feldstein's original estimate suggested a huge decrease in private saving—about 38 percent—and a 20 percent decrease in gross national product over what it would have been in the absence of Social Security. This amounts, Feldstein noted, "to nearly 30 percent of consumer spending, more than twice the individual income tax payment, and substantially more than twice the level of national defense expenditures."

Thus, even if Social Security has had but a fraction of the effect that Feldstein originally estimated, it would still substantially curtail private capital formation. Even after subtracting any intrafamily, intergenerational transfers (taking the Barro effect into account) to obtain the net impact of the Social Security system, it is likely that the effects would still be enormous, given the gigantic size of the Social Security system. A variety of additional econometric estimates have been presented by Feldstein and his coauthors as well as by other people. A mistake in the original generation of Feldstein's data was noted by Leimer and Lesnoy, who reestimated with the corrected data and concluded that there is no evidence that Social Security has affected private saving.[10] Feldstein then redid his studies and came to more or less his original conclusion: Social Security has a substantial impact on saving.[11]

All of the numerous additional papers on this subject cannot be reviewed here,[12] but my interpretation of the econometric evidence to date is as follows. There is modest proof that Social Security has had a direct effect in depressing private saving; the evidence, however, is far from conclusive. There is still much debate on such points as the proper specification of a consumption function, the proper specification and measurement of Social Security wealth, and the proper sample period to be examined. It is also clear that care must be taken in interpreting evidence to allow for private intrafamily, intergenerational offsets. As I have indicated, the documentation available on this issue is quite meager, but my working judgment is that Social Security has had a depressing effect on private saving, although not nearly so large as the dollar-for-dollar substitution implied in Feldstein's original work. A good working hypothesis would place the substitution between 25 and 50 cents per dollar.

Thus, the growth of Social Security may have had the unintended consequence of distorting saving decisions. It has affected labor markets by inducing people to retire earlier than they otherwise would, and it has impaired overall growth by dampening private saving and investment. From the standpoint of economic efficiency, then, Social Security leaves much to be desired.

IMPACT ON INSURANCE

The provision of hospital and disability insurance by the Social Security system interacts with retirement planning. For example, one major reason people save is to help insure against illness; hospital insurance could reduce this incentive. But if Social Security has induced artificial distortions in retirement and saving decisions, it has helped to resolve some of the adverse selection problems in annuity markets and health insurance. On balance, these effects have probably been quite important.

Still, the method by which hospital insurance, for example, is provided is not particularly efficient. In fact, the system of coinsurance and the nature of reimbursement have led many researchers to conclude that too much insurance has been provided for some health-care needs and not enough for others. The most important type of insurance to provide is that covering catastrophic events that could lead to a substantial reduction in a family's standard of living. While proposals for such insurance surface, on occasion, in the United States, our current Medicare system does not fully insure against catastrophes. I share with Martin Feldstein, Victor Fuchs, and Alain Enthoven the belief that coinsurance rates should be raised in Medicare and that much more of the spending should be concentrated on insuring against major catastrophes as opposed to cost sharing for minor illnesses.[13] In fact, even for the elderly poor, some form of cost sharing may be necessary. The basic problem is that if the cost is reduced to a small fraction of a dollar for each dollar usage, the available resources are not effectively rationed, and instead substantially more medical care—not all of it necessarily health improving—will be induced.

ADMINISTRATIVE EFFICIENCY AND SIMPLICITY

Is the current Social Security system doing all that it can to satisfy efficiency norms with regard to administrative expenses and private compliance costs? I do not think so. As a fraction of total outlays, Social Security administration costs are in line with those of other major institutions in the United States and are probably lower than those of corresponding institutions in other societies. But the incredible expansion of coverage and the increasing complexity of and changes in rules and regulations have brought major problems. For example, the Social Security Administration is several years behind in transcribing earnings records. One major recommendation of President Reagan's Advisory Panel on Social Security was to provide funds for capital improvements in computer technology for the Social Security Administration, one of several expenditure increases necessary to improve efficiency.

For a large fraction of the population in the United States, Social Security represents their major insurance. Their own insurance planning and knowledge, therefore, depend heavily on the information they have available about their prospective Social Security benefits. Despite the enormous importance of Social Security to the typical American family, however, little public information is available. The cost to the private sector in dealing with Social Security is unnecessarily large.

The calculation of an individual's potential disability, survivors, or retirement benefits under Social Security is an enormously complicated task that requires accountants, actuaries, and computer programs. The Social Security Administration will not compute information for specific individuals until they become eligible for one of the benefit coverages or until they reach age 59. But does it make sense for households headed, for example, by someone age 55 not to know what Social Security insurance coverages and potential retirement benefits to expect?

Those covered by private pensions are accustomed to receiving annual statements outlining their contributions, their entitlements under specific contingencies, and so on. The failure of our Social Security system to provide this information is simply a disgrace. How can private insurance and saving be intelligently planned without knowledge of what is available under Social Security? This problem is heightened by the growing number of private pensions that are "integrated" with Social Security—i.e., that contain clauses whereby overall benefits are determined by a formula that reduces the private pension benefit based on the amount of Social Security received. Thus, it is even difficult to know what private benefits to expect because it is not known how much is obtainable under Social Security. The dissemination of specific information necessary for retirement planning should be given a high priority and is an efficiency norm that the Social Security system in the United States fails.

TARGET EFFECTIVENESS

What about the target effectiveness of the Social Security system? Does Social Security provide the types of coverage that people really require? Does it finance them effectively? Do the sums go to people who really need them? Is everyone getting a fair deal on their contributions?

As pointed out earlier, the Social Security system has always been a compromise between the twin goals of earned income support and social adequacy. Therefore, the benefit formula has always been loosely tied to previous contributions but tilted toward a higher replacement rate for low-income workers, at least as measured by their average covered monthly earnings. Recall the five basic types of coverage and benefits provided by Social Security, and it immediately becomes clear that some mistargeting has occurred.

If the Social Security system is viewed as a kind of social insurance, it seems strange that individuals without spouses or dependent children are—by contributing to the general financial resources available—financing spousal and survivors benefits. Of course, people might be single currently but prospectively could have a spouse and/or children. However, these various types of coverages are not very well targeted.

Another question about the target effectiveness of Social Security concerns the nature of the transfer and annuity components of the payroll tax. As discussed earlier, over three fourths of benefit payments can be interpreted as a general transfer from taxpayers. Is this general transfer from taxpayers targeted to people who really need it? Is this income providing substantial transfers to individuals who do not need it?

Social Security gets a mixed scorecard on this issue. While Social Security is the single most important contributor to the enormous reduction of poverty among the elderly in the United States, this achievement has come at an enormous cost. Remember that whenever benefits have been increased, they have been increased across the board (including when they are indexed for inflation). Thus, the earlier huge increases in Social Security benefits went to retired millionaires as well as to retired poor people. Is it not possible to match outlays more closely to contributions and to need?

SOCIAL SECURITY AND EQUITY: WHO GETS HOW GOOD A DEAL?

Of the many problems plaguing the Social Security system, the problem of differential treatment of individuals and families in different situations is the one that engenders the strongest reaction. A substantial number of groups within the population claim they are being treated unfairly. For example, married working women claim that they are being penalized because, while many of them pay Social Security taxes, they get no additional sum above and beyond their spouse's benefit (which they would get even if they were not employed) when they retire. Couples in which only one partner earns income receive 50 percent more

Table 4.1
Who Gets How Good a Deal From Social Security?
The Age Structure of Transfers

Panel A		
Age (in 1984)	Present Value of (expected) Benefits less Taxes (average per family)	Transfers as Percentage of Total Benefits
72+	$69,000	89%
62-71	45,000	64
52-61	36,000	45
42-51	31,000*	32
32-41	21,200*	18
under 32	16,000*	17

than an individual with the same payment history. Given identical earnings histories, males and females are treated symmetrically with respect to their benefit formula, but, of course, their earnings histories are not identical. Further, some women are systematically excluded from Social Security provisions because of marital dissolution and their lack of sharing in the earned income credits accrued by their spouses.

Finally, and by far the most critical issue in terms of equity, is that individuals and families of different ages fare unequally under the Social Security system.† Those who have retired in the past and who are soon to retire receive substantially more than they and their employers paid in plus any reasonable real rate of interest. On the other hand, some of those who are in the early stages of their careers can look forward to receiving substantially less than what they and their employers pay in plus reasonable interest. For example, on average, in 1940, a 65-year-old male had "paid" for only 2.3 percent of the benefits he would receive; the

---

† Results among studies are not directly comparable because of the use of different discount rates, current or outdated life-expectancy tables, etc.

Table 4.1 (*concluded*)

Panel B

	Year in which Head of Household Becomes Age Sixty-Five				
	1970	1980	1995	2010*	2025*
Projected internal rate of return for married couples with median earnings history for primary worker, none for spouse	8.5%	5.9	3.6	2.5	2.2

*1983 Amendments main effect is to worsen the "deal" for younger individuals for two reason: (1) taxation of benefits will gradually reduce (net) benefits more and more through time because the exemption levels are not indexed; (2) the increase in the retirement age for full benefits to sixty-six in 2005 and to sixty-seven in 2022 will reduce the present value of benefits paid to those retiring after those dates.

Source: Panel A updated from M. Boskin, M. Avrin, and K. Cone, "Modelling Alternative Solutions to the Long-Run Social Security Financing Problem," in M. Feldstein, ed., *Behavioral Simulation Methods in Tax Policy Analysis* (Chicago: University of Chicago Press, 1983). Panel B from M. Hurd and J. Shoven, "The Distributional Impact of Social Security," in D. Wise, ed., *Pensions, Labor and Individual Choice* (Chicago: University of Chicago Press, 1985) and author's calculations.

rest was a pure transfer, a welfare payment. But this transfer percentage has been decreasing. On average, in 1970, those retiring at age 65 paid 32 percent of the benefits they would receive. The primary point is that different individuals and families receive vastly different "deals" in the sense that the ratio of benefits received to taxes paid varies. This situation occurs for a number of reasons including the progressive benefit formula, minimum benefit, spousal benefits, the different periods of coverage, differential life expectancies, etc. Table 4.1 presents some preliminary analysis of how good a deal different age groups get from Social Security based on two different studies using complementary methods and data, by the author updating an early paper and by my research colleagues, Michael Hurd and John Shoven. The unmistakable differences in benefits by age group are pronounced and dramatic. While those already retired and soon to retire lived through the Depression and have lower lifetime incomes than current workers are likely to have, on average, it is clear they received a tremendous deal from Social Security— much better than they could have had in any private system. But for those age 40 or younger (or about 50 and younger subsequent to the changes in the 1983 Amendments), the deal from Social Security in expected present value terms turns worse or even negative under certain circumstances.[14] Remember, though, that the absence of actuarially fair annuities markets indicates that households may value Social Security benefits more than the expected present value of the benefits, because of the provision of insurance against the uncertain date of death. In any event, the vastly different treatment of different age groups shown in Table 4.1 dispels the myth that Social Security is providing identical treatment to all groups in the population.

Table 4.2 demonstrates that the quality of the Social Security deal varies by income class. For example, while the percentage of the benefits received in the form of a transfer declines slightly as an individual moves up the income scale, the actual dollars increase. Those above the maximum covered earnings, for the period under consideration when they were working, receive more than any of the other classes. Hurd and Shoven recorded a similar result. Thus, despite the tilt in the benefit formula and a higher replacement rate for lower income groups, as an individual moves up the income scale, the transfers received increase substantially.

Table 4.3 indicates a variety of ways in which Social Security benefits can differ depending on marital status and whether an individual is male or female. For instance, a one-earner couple gets a substantial net subsidy ($14,375 for a couple with the husband working), whereas a single male at the same income level ($30,000) pays $56,000 more in taxes than he receives in benefits. Are these different treatments sensible or capricious? Are they the result of historical accidents or desirable social policy?

The fulfillment of the desire for efficiency and equity in Social Security is tied up with the conflict between its twin objectives:

Table 4.2
Who Gets How Good a Deal from Social Security?
The Intracohort Transfers by Income Class

A. *Projected Transfers by income quartiles for current middle-aged workers (in their fifties), in 1984 dollars*

Lowest quartile	Second lowest	Second highest	Highest
$41,600	$43,600	$42,100	$45,200

B. *Estimated median transfers by wealth quartile, 1969, for sixty-two-year-olds (expressed in 1968 dollars)*

Lowest quartile	Second lowest	Second highest	Highest
$10,626	$15,809	$16,997	$18,135

Source: Panel A updated from M. Boskin, M. Avrin, and K. Cone, "Modelling Alternative Solutions to the Long-Run Social Security Financing Problem," in M. Feldstein, ed., *Behavioral Simulation Methods in Tax Policy Analysis* (Chicago: University of Chicago Press, 1983). Panel B calculation by M. Hurd and J. Shoven, "The Distributional Impact of Social Security," in D. Wise, ed., *Pensions, Labor and Individual Choice* (Chicago: University of Chicago Press, 1985), based on Retirement History Survey data for 1969.

earned benefits and income adequacy. Most critics of the program would reform it in the direction of one objective or the other. I propose separating the transfer and annuity goals. This is necessary in order to provide a more target-effective and cost-conscious provision of benefits; it is also likely to provide an opportunity to reduce Social Security's long-term deficit.

Under my proposal, all workers would be accorded the *same* rate of return under Social Security's annuity program. The inequities that undermine support for the system would be eliminated in the sense that every family and individual would receive an identical return on his contribution. It must be emphasized, however, that young people may not receive the same rate of return they could get on private investment because of the enormous

Table 4.3
Who Gets How Good a Deal from Social Security?
The Effects of Marital Status and Sex*

	Net Projected Transfers in 1983				
	One-Earner Couple		Two-Earner Couple	Single Individual	
1982 Earnings Total	Husband Worker	Wife Worker		Male	Female
$15,000	28,218	30,947	3,318	-21,321	-4,384
$30,000	14,375	17,854	-24,808	-56,347	-32,673

* Example for individuals age forty in 1983.

Source: A. Pellechio and G. Goodfellow, "Individual Gains and Losses from Social Security Before and After the 1983 Amendments," *Cato Journal*, Fall, 1983.

long-term deficit facing Social Security. If the shortfall is not funded elsewhere—i.e., outside the Social Security system—the "deal" that Social Security provides them will be actuarially identical but somewhat less than fair. But there is no way around this problem. If Social Security is to operate as an actuarially fair system, it will be necessary to raise other taxes, and the combination of Social Security and other taxes will be unfair. *There is no free lunch.* We cannot make Social Security financially solvent without either cutting benefits or raising taxes.

SOCIAL SECURITY AND FINANCIAL FEASIBILITY

In addition to the problems of efficiency and equity in the Social Security system is the most critical question: financial feasibility. Can the Social Security system accomplish what it is intended to do?

Several different methods have been used to estimate the extent of the financial insolvency lurking ahead. The Social Security Administration usually quotes income and outgo as fractions of taxable payroll, or of gross national product, over alternative periods. But, because of discounting and aggregation problems, this method makes it difficult to understand the financial dimension. Benefits under current law, year by year for the next 75 years, and revenues under various assumptions about economics and demographics, were estimated in the long-term forecast of the trustees of the Social Security Administration and in my own projections. These estimates were then discounted back to the present at a real interest rate (usually about 2.1 percent) and the differences examined. This calculation is the source of the $1.8 trillion deficit I had forecast in the Old-Age, Survivors, and Disability Insurance program and the several trillion dollar gap in Hospital Insurance prior to the 1983 Amendments. If estimates were made for when the baby boom generation retires in, say, 2020, we would need many trillions of dollars more—even ignoring the adjustment of these dollars for inflation.

An alternative procedure, based on what the Social Security Administration calls a "closed group" analysis, has been used in various documents that have appeared in the press, in books, and even at the back of the *Economic Report of the President.* Closed group analysis takes the benefits and taxes of all current adults, projects them into the future for some period, and compares the difference discounted to the present. This procedure implies that *all* future tax increases will be paid by those who are *not yet adults;* it excludes those who are going to be working in future years but are not yet born and therefore is very misleading.

The closed group estimate has been defended on the ground that it is an appraisal of the price at which people would be willing to sell their promise of future Social Security benefits. I am sure many younger workers would be prepared to receive far less than this amount in order to eliminate the uncertainty of how much they will receive. In any event, the closed group deficit is much larger than the open group 75-year numbers I have presented.

I think that the $1.8 trillion figure was the most reasonable calculation to use in dealing with the long-term financial solvency of Social Security's retirement and disability program. While it is conservatively estimated using intermediate assumptions, it is probably the best number for planning purposes. It simply says that, either today or 10 years from now, or gradually over 50 years, or on the eve of the baby boom generation's retirement, the equivalent number of dollars (adjusted for inflation and interest) will have to be achieved in benefit reductions or in tax increases in order to make Social Security financially feasible. This is what the 1983 Social Security Amendments were designed to raise, although, as explained in Chapter 1, they almost certainly will fail to do so.

Since the way we choose to deal with the future financial burden of Social Security—both with respect to changes in benefits and taxes and with regard to the timing of these changes—has substantial bearing on the well-being of various groups in the population, the basic question is who will pay for what? Suppose, at one extreme, we simply wait until the deficits become severe in the next century and raise taxes then. Suppose, at the other extreme, we raise taxes now in order to keep benefits the same without increasing taxes in the future. While in each case the benefits do not change, the distribution of payment for them varies markedly. If taxes are raised now, those in their 50s who are still working will pay considerably more; if taxes are not raised substantially until 2020, those under the age of 35 will bear the entire direct burden of the tax increase, and those over the age of 35 will escape paying. In either case, the total tax increases will be considerable, amounting to several trillion dollars.

Or consider changes in benefits that would bring the system into financial solvency given current projected tax revenues. We could wait until early in the next century and make substantial cuts in benefits then; alternatively, we could begin to do something about benefit growth now, although changes might not take effect fully for several years. These two alternatives would have very different effects from the ones noted above. First, Social Security benefits would be lower. Assuming the second scenario, people soon to retire would receive slightly smaller benefits; this reduction in the growth of benefits would gradually increase through time, so that, when the baby boom generation retires, the benefits will have grown more slowly and hence would be lower than if no benefit changes occur. Second, substantially less taxes will be necessary to support Social Security. The burden of bringing the system into financial solvency will be borne across the board—partly by those retiring between now and the baby boom generation's retirement, partly by the baby boom generation in their retirement, and partly by the children of the baby boom generation.

The real issues are, it seems, how we will ultimately pay for benefits that we decide we want and need to provide and how we move from the current structure of taxes and benefits to a more rational and efficient system. Any proposal that deals with how changing taxes or benefits affect a particular group is always *ambiguous* because it does not define *how* the current system will be brought into financial balance. Since abrupt changes can be quite disruptive and since no plausible variations in demographics or the economy will prevent the financial crisis in the Social Security system from occurring, consensus on a sensible solution should be sought now.

Fortunately, there may be one area in which the goals of economic efficiency, equity, and financial feasibility converge: gradually phasing out excess, or transfer, payments to nonpoor elderly retirees. This step, in and of itself, by eliminating welfare for the rich, will considerably reduce the Social Security deficit and move the system toward more modest size and target effectiveness.

CONCLUSION

Through the transfer of resources from richer younger workers to older poorer retirees, Social Security has done a lot to prevent destitution among the elderly. But the system is not working in as target-effective and as cost-conscious a manner as desirable.

I recommend that the following reforms be seriously considered:

1. The substantial welfare provided by Social Security to the rich should be phased out.
2. The considerable disparities in the treatment of different groups in the population—based on age, sex, marital status, and income class—should be eliminated. A separate program, based solely on *need,* should augment the basic Social Security program in which everyone should receive an *identical* actuarial return on his lifetime contributions (and those of his employer).
3. The various disability and health-care provisions must be coordinated—not dealt with piecemeal—to ensure efficiency, equity, simplicity, and financial solvency. For ex-

ample, health expenditures are a substantial fraction of expenditures for many elderly, and disability is an alternative to retirement benefits for some people.

4. We must address now the basic problems plaguing our public system of support for retirees. In order to facilitate retirement planning and to prevent major disruptions, a program must be phased in gradually after a grace period. That means we must begin to come to grips now with *how* we are going to provide *what* benefits at *whose* expense. Drifting along without an answer to this question merely postpones the inevitable and will make dealing with the financial issue more difficult, more disruptive, and more costly. We need not be saddled with an inefficient, inequitable, and financially insolvent system into the next century.

CHAPTER 5

Changing the Scope of Social Security

INTRODUCTION

During Social Security's first four decades, rapid economic growth, strong labor force expansion, and public support for this program—despite the fact that it led to increases in taxes—all contributed to a general growth of revenues and periodic surpluses in the Social Security "trust funds." As surpluses developed, politicians looked for "good" things to do with the funds. After all, it was argued, there was no need to build up huge balances because future taxes would pay future benefits. Further, those opposed to maintaining large surpluses claimed—adopting the notion attributed to J. M. Keynes—that an excess supply of total saving would be deleterious to overall economic performance and would induce recession. Thus, the revenue growth and surpluses led to a natural and politically painless increase in benefit levels and extension of coverage.[1]

The issue now is whether we can expect the sources of revenues out of which benefit growth was financed—i.e., increases in population, productivity, and the labor force—to be able to contribute nearly as much "painless" revenue in the future and what changes in the scope of Social Security are likely to occur for ideological or financial reasons. Some argue for universal coverage or for including various groups currently not part of the Social Security system. Many others argue that the government never should have gotten involved or it should only have mandated private coverage that could be "purchased" from a large number of, say, insurance companies. The larger the scope of Social Security in terms of coverage, benefit levels, and types of protection, the smaller will be the demand for private insurance. Thus, the issue of the sensible scope of the system really entails balancing the advantages of free choice and competition against the difficulties that arise in providing actuarially fair annuities in the capital market and in guaranteeing a minimally acceptable level of retirement income for those who are improvident or unlucky.

THE DIFFICULTIES OF FUNDING
FUTURE BENEFITS

Undoubtedly, a major impetus for the growth in Social Security benefits and in coverage has been the desire to improve the security and well-being of the elderly, who, until recently, have been disproportionately poor. But, historically, benefits have been raised across the board, not targeted to those truly in need. (See Appendix A for a detailed discussion of the history and nature of Social Security benefits.)

How were these substantial benefit increases financed? Since Social Security was funded on a pay-as-you-go basis, they were paid for by the growth of Social Security tax revenues, which increased for a number of reasons: the growth of the labor force, the rise in average earnings, the extension of coverage, and increase in the taxable maximum wage base.

It is easiest to understand the potential long-term return that would be provided in a Social Security program by first thinking of an economy with a stable population and a stable labor force whose only source of general income growth occurs through the increased productivity of workers. Suppose such an economy has a constant rate of productivity growth of g percent per year. If that is the case, at constant tax rates, revenues will rise g percent per year. If retirement patterns also remain stable, the same tax rates can be applied to a growing tax base to provide higher benefits, although the ratio of wages to benefits will remain constant.

Now suppose the population also grows, say, at a constant rate of n percent per year. With stable labor force participation rates, retirement patterns, life expectancy, and so on, the tax base against which payroll taxes are levied rises at approximately the sum of the population and productivity growth rates—i.e., $n + g$. Thus, rising benefits are possible, although per capita benefits will remain constant relative to real wages. Since the retired population as well as the working population grows at rate n, benefits per capita grow at rate g, the rate of growth of real wages, and thus the ratio of benefits to real wages, is constant. The growth rate g is already included in the formula for computing benefits (since earnings histories are indexed by wage growth), so *further legislated* increases in benefits are unwarranted.

Assume, however, that demographic changes alter the ratio of workers to retirees. For example, suppose there is a substantial bulge in the number of workers relative to retirees—e.g., an increase in the labor force participation of second wage earners in families (usually wives). *Temporarily,* therefore, the ratio of tax revenue to the total number of retirees will rise (assuming that tax rates remain constant). Or, alternatively, consider the case in which the population's growth rate is not constant but instead surges, such as occurred in the post-World War II baby boom. This circumstance also will create a situation where, ceteris paribus, growing benefits can be financed at constant tax rates *for awhile*. However, neither of these forms of increases in tax revenues can sustain a *continually* growing level of benefits as opposed to a once-and-for-all increase.

Of course, the simplistic suppositions about the potential sources of funding for growing Social Security benefits can be augmented by increasing the tax rates. Traditionally, this has occurred in two ways: raising the "contribution" rates for employers and employees and raising the maximum taxable wage base. For example, when Social Security was set up in 1937, only the first $3,000 of earnings was taxable, and the rate was 1 percentage point each for employers and employees.[2] By 1985, the first $39,600 of earnings was being taxed at a contribution rate of 7.05 percent each, or 14.1 percent in total. Social Security tax rates are scheduled to rise to 15.3 percent in total in 1990, and the annual maximum taxable earnings is scheduled to increase automatically with wages.

Two of the possible sources of extra tax revenue to finance the growth of Social Security benefits—real income growth (i.e., growth generated by productivity gains) and population growth—can sustain a *continually* rising benefit level with constant tax rates. But the growth in the labor force obviously has an upper limit. For example, the female labor force participation rate has climbed from 33 percent only a couple of decades ago to over 50 percent today. Eventually, the percentage of women who work in the marketplace, and are able to do so, will reach a maximum at a participation rate in any given calendar year well under 100 percent. (The figure commonly used by the Social Security Administration for the eventual maximum female labor force participation rate is 72 percent.) In the transition to this higher labor force participation level for women, some modest growth in revenues will be temporarily available as more workers are taxed, but once the upper limit is reached, no further gains will be available. The same occurs when there is a temporary bulge in the population due to an increase in the birth rate. The opposite occurs when there is a decline in the fertility rate—such as recently in the United States, where the total fertility rate has sunk below the 2.1 percent necessary to maintain a growing population—a situation that does not bode well for the future ratio of retirees to workers.

Table 5.1
Basic Trends Contributing to Growth in Social Security Revenues*

	Proportion Jobs Covered	Percent Wages Taxable	Female Labor Force Participation Rate	Productivity Growth Rate **	Fertility Rate
1950	61%	56%	33%	6 %	-
1960	86	65	38	3	3.6
1970	89	68	43	2.5	2.4
1980	90	80	51	0.9	1.8
1981	under 90	80	53	0.8	1.9
2000 ***	-	-	72	1.5	2.0

* Besides increases in tax rates and maximum taxable earnings.

** Average over preceding five years.

*** Projected.

Sources: U.S. Senate, Committee on Finance, *Social Security Financing*, December 1982; 1983 Social Security Administration Trustees Report; and *Economic Report of the President*, 1984.

Table 5.1 shows some basic data on the trends in female labor force participation, the growth of productivity and real wages, and so on. It is clear from these numbers that the conditions that caused Social Security revenue to increase are not expected to continue into the future. The extra revenues being contributed by the baby boomers and the growing number of women in the labor force will soon be exhausted, and, unless fertility rates rise, our population growth rate will begin to slow.[3]

Add to these trends the increased life expectancy and early retirement documented in Chapters 2 and 3, and it becomes clear that temporary reversals—analogous to the temporary gains provided by increased labor force participation rates—can occur. In terms of its impact on the benefit level per recipient, a steadily rising life expectancy is much like a decline in the growth rate of productivity (unless accompanied by later retirement). The trend toward early retirement undoubtedly is going to continue for awhile, but it is likely to level off. It may even reverse itself when the combination of improved medical care, greater life expectancy, recent antidiscrimination legislation, and less stringent compulsory retirement laws work their way through the system.

These data and tendencies reveal a startling fact, however. While Social Security revenue increases were financed partly out of higher tax rates on a larger tax base, to a great extent extra revenues were generated by the growth of the labor force, which occurred because of circumstances that will not be sustainable very much longer and that are being partly offset by increases in the length of the retirement period.

Therefore, the major hope for increasing Social Security revenues while maintaining constant tax rates is for higher rates of productivity growth. But, as shown in Table 5.1, the Social Security Administration trustees are not terribly optimistic about our long-term productivity growth rate as compared to the increases experienced in the quarter century after World War II. If there is a substantial increase in productivity growth, it will be a great boon to Social Security, as well as to the economy in general. But, as discussed, part of the decline in productivity growth is due to the decline in capital formation, which, in turn, partly reflects decreases in our saving rate, which, in turn, may be affected by the growth in Social Security. We are on the horns of a dilemma. Substantial increases in the level and nature of Social Security benefits may lead to further reductions in the supply of capital available for productive investment, which is one of the sources of growing productivity.

From the evidence presented, it would be impossible not to reach the conclusion that it will be increasingly difficult to fund the types of Social Security benefits currently being promised without enormous tax increases.

There is, though, one commonly suggested route to "save" Social Security whenever it runs into the funding crises it continually creates; that is, to mandate universal coverage or the extension of coverage beyond those already protected. But participation has already reached a point where even mandating universal coverage would provide only a modest one-time increase in revenues. Approximately half of state and local government employees, and federal employees unaffected by the 1983 Amendments, are the only remaining large groups in the labor force that are not covered by Social Security—just a small percentage of the labor force. While the revenue gained through their participation would help, it would not make a significant difference.

Regardless of the actual amount of revenue raised, though, it might well be argued that—for equity reasons—these exempt individuals ought to share in financing the Social Security short-fall and in improving Social Security's long-term financial sol-vency. But the only way to bring them into the system is to include them on an *actuarially unfair basis*. If we bring them in on an actuarially fair basis, the present value of the benefits received will equal the present value of the taxes paid, plus interest, and there-fore there will be *no* contribution to Social Security's long-term financial solvency. But if we attempt to bring them in on less than an actuarially fair basis, they undoubtedly would oppose partici-pation in the system. Politically, requiring state employees to par-ticipate in a federal pension system is a sticky issue, involving questions of constitutional and states' rights.

The remaining avenue to be explored for raising additional revenues for Social Security would be a massive opening of the floodgates to new immigrants. But, again, while this move would provide a cash infusion as these people found employment and paid Social Security taxes, it would only contribute to the system's long-run financial solvency if they too were brought in on an actuarially unfair basis. And since the current benefit formula is highly tilted toward low-income and lower-middle-income house-holds and toward families with many dependents, it is likely that allowing for increased immigration—particularly from Latin America, as is most often discussed in the United States—would, if anything, make the situation worse.

In summary then, *continuing to provide growing Social Security benefits will be economically and politically costly.* The modest gains in Social Security revenue expected from increases in female labor force participation and the wage gains made by the baby boom generation will be offset by increases in life expectancy. Even completely removing the taxable maximum wage base and taxing all covered earnings would not help very much since over 90 percent of earnings in covered employment are already subject to Social Security tax. Extending the scope of the system to universal coverage in order to obtain revenues from groups not now cov-ered will not aid greatly in solving Social Security's long-run fi-nancial problems. Tax rates will have to rise if higher levels of

Social Security benefits are to be provided. And, as noted in Chapter 1, the tax rates necessary to finance projected benefit growth are enormous, possibly double current levels.

Rethinking the benefit side of Social Security—the types of coverage provided, the level of real benefits, and the distribution of benefits among families by various measures of need—also is necessary if we are to finance retirement income in a more cost-effective manner. Various means tests for auxiliary benefits already have been proposed in some West European countries.

But there is another idea to consider. There are those who think we ought to junk the Social Security system entirely. These people argue that Social Security never should have been a public system in the first place—that we should have relied on private provision for retirement income, hospital care, etc., from the beginning. At the very least, these people argue, the current working generation ought to be given the choice of opting out of Social Security and providing for their own retirement—for example, by putting funds into individual retirement accounts. Of course, this solution raises all sorts of difficulties. Those who would have the greatest incentive to leave the system would be those for whom it is the worst projected deal. Allowing these people to opt out of Social Security at a time when it is facing a long-term financial crisis of enormous magnitude would mean knowingly increasing the relative burden for taxpayers remaining within the system. Nevertheless, the search for a solution to Social Security's problems must include a consideration of privatization—the option for private versus public provision of social insurance—a subject to which we now turn.

PRIVATIZATION OF SOCIAL SECURITY

Sometimes the argument for complete privatization of Social Security—i.e., totally removing the federal government from any role in the provision of old-age insurance—is based on political ideology that suggests government programs are bad *a priori* and that an individual might receive "higher rates of return" on investments in the private capital market. This argument, however, can be quite misleading. First, switching from our present system to a private one would mean that the current generation of taxpayers would finance two retirement systems: *one for the currently elderly population and one—a genuine trust fund—for their own retirement.* This would approximately double taxes and private contributions for these households. Further, the calculations usually presented assume unrealistic rates of return—adjusted for inflation—on long-term private investment. For example, Peter Ferrara assumes that the return to the economy from the extra investment generated by private capital formation would be so large as to be able to pay for the switch.[4] But, based on historical experience, such estimates are well out of the reasonable range.

Still another problem with complete privatization is that private insurance markets have difficulty providing actuarially fair annuities. One reason for this is that, because of the problem of adverse selection of risk, actuarially fair insurance markets simply do not exist. The adverse selection problem could be avoided, though, if one large pool or group were formed so that individuals could not opt out. Social Security roughly accomplishes this goal. Compulsory provision of insurance through the private sector could accomplish approximately the same result as long as individuals and households were randomly assigned to firms and market mechanisms were not the exclusive means of allocation.

Another significant difficulty with privatization arises from the fact that we do not have indexed bonds in our society. The federal government's failure to offer inflation-indexed bonds is a disgrace for a variety of reasons, but this shortcoming is particularly onerous with respect to retirement income planning. While insurance companies and other financial intermediaries have improved their annuities by tying yields to interest rates in the market—thereby providing a better inflation hedge than was previously available—there is no guarantee that fluctuations in market rates will exactly offset inflation.

Inflation and expected inflation are only two of many determinants of market interest rates. In the 1970s, for example, interest rates not infrequently fell below the rate of inflation, and, more recently, real interest rates (the interest rate minus the inflation rate) have soared to unprecedented levels of 7 percent or more. Thus, the lack of indexed bonds is a major problem for the elderly attempting to guarantee themselves a steady level of real income to finance a steady consumption flow during retirement.

But neither adverse selection nor the lack of indexed bonds is a sufficient reason to perpetuate the type of Social Security system we have today in the United States. As private markets improve with respect to their ability to provide actuarially fair annuities and as the federal government considers other policies (such as the provision of indexed bonds), the case for a large publicly financed annuity program will weaken. Even now, while the fact that actuarially fair annuities and inflation-indexed bonds are unavailable has a significant impact on those with modest income levels, these issues become less critical as an individual moves up the income scale. Replacement of public provision by compulsory private coverage should be considered. Short of *complete* privatization, a variety of intervening levels and forms of private provision of old-age insurance also deserves serious attention.

It is clear that Social Security's growth beyond provision for basic minimum needs has threatened to crowd out the legitimate function of private provision for insurance. In addition, the current level of Social Security coverage and benefits may be excessive—except for those at the bottom of the income scale. Gradually slowing the growth of Social Security benefits for middle- and upper-income elderly individuals is desirable, even if there were no impending financial crisis in the Social Security system.

Thus, it is important to build toward a system that *preserves incentives for private insurance, saving, pensions, and intrafamily transfers above and beyond the basic first layer of support provided by Social Security.* Given the current unavailability of actuarially fair annuities and inflation-indexed bonds, Social Security plays a legitimate social function in providing this first layer of support. But this should not be an excuse for completely socializing all provision for retirement, disability, and related contingencies. A sensible balance must be reached. I am somewhat in sympathy with those who would like to privatize *part* of *some* of the components of Social Security beyond minimally adequate coverage.

Arguing that complete privatization is unwise and impractical and that some social insurance system is desirable—while maintaining that the current system is neither cost conscious nor target-effective—leaves a substantial gray area into which the "proper" mix (which benefits in what amounts should be publicly provided) might fall. It also should be kept in mind that, in addition to traditional forms of private saving and direct purchase of insurance, employer prepaid health insurance programs and private pension programs in firms are increasingly available. While it is not the purpose of this volume to go into great detail about the nature of these private pension plans, a few important points are worth noting.

Almost half of the United States' labor force is covered by private or state and local government pensions—two-and-a-half times the percentage covered three decades ago. About three quarters of the participants are enrolled in defined-benefit plans (plans that target a fraction of salary as ultimate benefits); the remainder subscribe to defined-contribution plans (plans that set a contribution rate out of salary and result in benefits tied exclusively to the returns from investing the contributions). But only about half of the participants are currently vested—i.e., have been at their jobs long enough to fully share in benefits. As of 1977, almost two out of every five participants in defined-benefit plans were in plans *integrated with Social Security*, and this trend toward integration is growing rapidly.[5]

This growth in private pensions has occurred for a variety of reasons including the increase in life expectancy, the tax advantages offered by private pensions as compared to other forms of savings and insurance, and the hedge offered by private pensions against uncertain Social Security benefits. Undoubtedly, population patterns, marital status, and other demographic factors also have played a significant role. The projections are that private pension plans will continue to grow, but, as the extent of integration with Social Security increases, a short-run *direct* offset will automatically occur. Unlike other forms of private saving, in the short run, private pension benefits will increase if Social Security benefits decrease.

To illustrate this idea, consider an example of a couple at retirement: the husband worked in a job covered by a defined-benefit pension, he is fully vested, and his wife never worked. Suppose the defined benefit is equal to 80 percent of the husband's salary in his final year of work, with the private plan supplementing Social Security up to this maximum amount. Suppose, also, taking a typical case, that Social Security replaces 50 percent of this individual's final year of earnings. Thus, the private pension plan is committed to providing 30 percent. Consider what happens, however, if the rate of Social Security benefit growth slows; the Social Security replacement rate falls slightly, and the private pension defined benefit rises automatically.

Therefore, in this as in many other cases, reductions in the growth of Social Security benefits will, in the short run, shift the cost in integrated plans directly onto the private pensions. In fact, this offset could be a substantial financial burden to these private plans, and some might go bankrupt if the benefit increases required of them were substantial.[6] Fortunately, when gradual changes are made in projected Social Security replacement rates, these changes can be incorporated into the pension planning of firms and workers, and the increase in defined benefits due to any decrease of Social Security benefit growth need not be dollar for dollar.

Thus, while complete privatization does not seem expedient, there are many intermediate proposals to "solve" the Social Security financing dilemma. Still, they all involve mandating or implicitly shifting costs onto the private sector in various degrees, rather than improving the efficiency of the public retirement income options.

CONCLUSION

While I have substantial sympathy for those who prefer to rely more heavily on private markets for social insurance and to limit the growth of Social Security benefits and coverage, privatization is impractical in that it would require the current generation of workers to pay twice: once for their own retirement and once to finance the benefits of those already retired—perhaps through the general income tax system. In addition, privatization is undesirable because, due to imperfections in capital markets, it cannot provide actuarially fair annuities.

On the other hand, I believe that the enormous growth in Social Security coverage and benefit levels has not been targeted very well. Wealthy individuals have received large benefits above and beyond what they and their employers paid in, plus interest, and are scheduled to do so for decades to come. The system also provides benefits to people who cannot use them—e.g., survivors' benefits to someone with no dependents or a spouse's benefit to single individuals. Since people are paying for things they are not getting and are not getting things for which they are paying, the overall system is inequitable, inefficient, and financially insolvent. But the performance of our Social Security system *can* be improved. At the same time, a larger role should be fashioned for the private provision of retirement income.

CHAPTER 6

Changes in Benefit Structure

INTRODUCTION

Various recommendations have been put forth to make the Social Security system more efficient, equitable, and financially solvent. The 1975 and 1979 reports of the President's Advisory Councils on Social Security, for example, proposed alternatives to the current benefit formula. Various Social Security reform proposals have been embodied in proposed legislation. Watered-down versions of some of these recommendations were included in the 1983 Social Security Amendments, which called for taxation of one half of Social Security benefits for wealthy retirees and a small gradual delayed increase in the age of eligibility for full benefits.

Basically, five types of suggestions have been made to slow the growth of Social Security benefits. These are:

1. Taxing benefits.
2. Changing the indexing formula so that real benefits do not remain constant with inflation.
3. Instituting various types of means tests—especially for auxiliary benefits—so that benefits are provided only to persons below certain specified income levels.
4. Changing the benefit formula itself.
5. Raising the age of eligibility for benefits.

Each of these proposals has its pros and cons as a partial solution, but none completely "solves" the basic problems plaguing the Social Security system.

TAXING BENEFITS

The taxation of Social Security benefits has been proposed numerous times over the years, including by the current author. But until the passage of the 1983 Social Security Amendments, this suggestion got nowhere. (In fact, it was defeated by the most lopsided votes in congressional history.) The unpopularity of this idea appears to be the result of politicians' fears that the taxation of benefits would be construed as a sharp reduction in benefits. But current benefits, as well as benefits that will be paid to future retirees, are not really based on an actuarially fair return on contributions; they are paid out of the taxes of current workers. In practice, because of the graduated structure of the personal income tax, the taxation of benefits would sharply increase the progressivity of the benefit formula. Under current law, as an individual moves up the income scale, his marginal personal income tax rate rises to a maximum of 50 percent. Thus, for the extremely wealthy, taxation of all Social Security benefits at the rate of 50 percent would be equivalent to reducing those benefits by one half. The revenue raised by taxing Social Security benefits under the personal income tax need not, but *could,* be credited to the Social Security system in order to help solve its financial problems. This, however, is a separate policy decision.

Many tax reformers have long argued that taxing some—or all—Social Security benefits is desirable from the standpoint of improving the equity of the income tax. Relative to other types of pensions, Social Security is given especially favorable tax treatment. The employee's contribution to Social Security (50 percent of the total due Social Security for that individual) is paid out of income already taxed; the employer's contribution for that individual is not included in gross earnings and is therefore not part of taxable income. Thus, half of Social Security benefits are doubly tax free, while taxes are paid only once on the other half. Compare this to the treatment of funds in an IRA or Keogh account or an employer prepaid pension. While the amount of money put into these pension accounts can be deducted from an individual's total taxable income in the year contributed—and therefore receives treatment similar to the employer's contribution to Social Security—the funds are taxable when they are disbursed during retirement. Thus, in order to place Social Security on an equal footing with private pensions, half of Social Security benefits would have to be taxable during retirement, or the employee contribution to Social Security would have to be tax exempt when paid and the entire benefit subject to personal income taxes during retirement.

These two strands of reform—one to make the benefit formula more progressive and the other to achieve more equitable treatment of taxable income—laid the groundwork for the measure, in the 1983 Social Security Amendments, to tax one half of the Social Security benefits of those individuals with incomes above $25,000 a year and of those married couples with incomes above $32,000 a year (various income sources were excluded). The income tax treatment of Social Security benefits is to be consistent with that of private pensions. It is expected that taxing one half of Social Security benefits will contribute about 0.6 percent of taxable payroll—about one third of the pre-1983 long-term deficit of Old-Age, Survivors, and Disability Insurance (OASDI).[1] Fully taxing Social Security benefits—by including them in adjusted gross income—would add 1.4 percent of taxable payroll to the long-term revenues of Social Security *if* the income taxes so received are credited to the Social Security funds.

While taxation of Social Security benefits has much to recommend it, it leaves a variety of problems unresolved. For example, while taxation of benefits would substantially reduce the payout to persons or families with high incomes, it would do nothing to match benefits to needs more closely. Single individuals who have never been married will still be subsidizing spouse's benefits for others; widows receiving survivors benefits will continue to collect them even after they remarry, *irrespective of their financial condition.* Thus, taxation of benefits may be a reasonable partial solution to some of Social Security's problems, but it does not help solve others.

CHANGING THE INDEXING FORMULA

In 1972, legislation introduced indexing—i.e., linking—Social Security benefits to inflation. But the original arrangement did not work properly; benefits were, in fact, *doubly* indexed as both increases in prices and increases in workers' earnings (which also tend to rise with the cost of living) were counted in the calculation of benefits. To compound the problem, there was high inflation in the 1970s. Beginning in 1977, in a gradual transition, the increases in wages were counted only prior to age 62, and then the primary insurance amount was indexed to price increases.[2] This double indexing, combined with the perception that the consumer price index (CPI) may have exaggerated the rate of inflation for the elderly compared to the nonelderly, appears to have overindexed Social Security benefits (increased them by more than true inflation) in the late 1970s.

A careful analysis by Michael Hurd and myself has led to the conclusion that there was some overindexing in the late 1970s and early 1980s, which led to a substantial overpayment—reaching a peak of $5 billion to $6 billion a year in the highest inflation years. But this was almost exclusively due to the excessive weight given to owner-occupied housing in the calculation of the CPI.[3] Revisions have been made in the CPI calculation to a rental equivalence measure of housing costs, which is now published regularly and is used to index Social Security. But when the annual inflation rate measures for the elderly are compared to those for the general population, *after correcting* for the mistreatment of housing in the original CPI figures, a startling conclusion emerges: for the past 20 years or so, the cumulative rise in cost of living was virtually identical for the general population and for the elderly—even though, as previously pointed out, the elderly have very different consumption patterns from the nonelderly. Because, in the course of inflation, prices for different commodities tend to rise at different rates, sharply different expenditure patterns could, in principle, give rise to very different inflation rates for the elderly and nonelderly. In the period under consideration, though, these different rates of price increase for different commodities canceled each other out. Still, there is no guarantee that this phenomenon will continue in the future.

In any event, the inflation of the late 1970s and early 1980s was accompanied by another startling development: prices rose more than wages. Usually it is the other way around—wages usually increase more than prices because of the growth in productivity. But real average hourly earnings declined in this period. Simply put, the general population had less real after-tax dollars to spend, while the elderly, at least in the Social Security component of their income, were fully protected against inflation. Because of this inequity, a variety of indexing adjustments have been proposed; for example, index only after the first 2 or 3 percentage points of inflation (i.e., the inflation adjustment would be the CPI increase minus 2 or 3 percent). In the short run, this type of arrangement would lead to a very small reduction in the rate of increase in Social Security benefits. But, cumulatively, over a long span of time, it would sharply reduce the real level of benefits relative to wages and the overall size of the Social Security system—all, more or less, across the board relative to income.

For example, under the 1983 Social Security Administration's assumptions, indexation at CPI minus 2 percentage points would reduce the present value of benefits (in real 1984 dollars) by over one trillion discounted 1985 dollars, from about $10 trillion to slightly under $9 trillion. Table 6.1 gives some details of this adjustment. As is evident, there is little impact on the net benefits of those already retired since they have already received most of their benefits and the CPI adjustment will affect them only in the few years of life they have left. But, for younger age groups, lowering the CPI adjustment reduces benefits substantially. For example, those under age 32 today would receive, over the next

Table 6.1
Effects of Indexing at CPI minus 2 Percent*

Age (in 1984)	Present Value of Benefits as % of Present Value under Current Law
72 or over	94%
62-71	87
52-61	83
42-51	84
32-41	84
under 32 (born by 1990)	82

* 1985 ff.

Source: Author's calculations.

75 years, only four fifths of the benefits in real present value terms as under current law. Thus, what might appear to be a sensible *short-term* way to deal with budgetary problems in times of severe inflation and with a perceived inequity in sharing the burdens imposed by the reduction of real wages, could—if frozen into law—result in drastic, although perhaps desirable, changes in the Social Security system.

While even a minor reduction in the indexing provisions could contribute much to the long-term solvency of Social Security, it would do nothing to make Social Security benefits more target effective; the CPI adjustment would be the same for those with different income levels, not based on need. Thus, before too long, those at the lower end of the income scale—despite having a higher replacement rate because of the current progressive nature of the benefit formula—would undoubtedly become candidates for a general assistance program. For the CPI minus 2 (or 3) percent proposals to make any sense, they must be periodically adjusted to account for the substantial erosion of benefits that occurs for those most in need. Further, they do nothing to remedy the poor targeting of auxiliary benefits.

INSTITUTING MEANS TESTS

Various types of means tests to ensure that benefits (especially auxiliary benefits) are paid only to those below specified income levels have been proposed from time to time. There has been substantial opposition to them, however. In part, this is because it is feared that means tests would lead to the infusion of general tax revenue funds and, in the short run, a larger Social Security program; in part, it is because the means test would transform the Social Security system into a "welfare" plan with all the stigma that word implies. I have some sympathy for this latter view. But the cost of Social Security has become so large that we can no longer afford not to call the substantial benefits, including the auxiliary allotments, what they really are: welfare—that is, transfer payments from the general population.

The United States supports the most costly system of benefits for spouses of any large advanced economy and the most generous benefits for surviving spouses.[4] Presumably, these auxiliary allowances were established because it was believed that spouses were dependent on the primary earner in the family. An expanding economy that, on occasion, generated large surpluses in Social Security provided the financing. But whatever the original rationale, the argument for supporting their continuation is weak; circumstances have changed dramatically in the United States. The assertion that everybody now "needs" these benefits is a dramatic overstatement considering the sharp increase in female labor force participation and the large decline in fertility rates. And, with a less vibrant economy, we simply can no longer afford to pay these excess benefits automatically. The horror stories of someone falling through the cracks of the social safety net are accompanied by corresponding ones of the wife of a retired millionaire whose benefits are increased by, say, 50 percent merely by virtue of being married. These benefits, it should be pointed out, are financed by much poorer general taxpayers.

There are some who believe that not only these auxiliary benefits but the entire Social Security program should be means tested. Some liberals would establish the means test at a very high level, thus creating a Social Security system that really is just a tax transfer system—one that provides *no additional* benefits for contributions beyond a modest amount. I believe that a cost-effective and humane "social adequacy" program is essential to Social Security and to the well-being of future generations of elderly Americans. Such a program could be expanded along the lines of the current Supplemental Security Income (SSI) program. It would ensure that anyone who, for whatever reason, was not covered would not fall through the cracks in the system and would have a decent standard of living in old age.

It is clear that, besides providing a basic, humane level of retirement support, the Social Security system has an additional role to play in financing earnings-related benefits. The problem is that the benefits ultimately received are imprecisely related to earnings and therefore to taxes paid. While the benefit formula calculates average indexed monthly earnings and is thereby related to taxes paid, the number of years included in the calculation, and the progressive structure of the benefit formula beyond provisions for social adequacy, break the link between benefits received and taxes paid. As a result, the system is open to the charge that people are being treated differently. If everyone received a common rate of return on their cumulative contributions to Social Security, *all* claims for additional benefits would *have to be based on need,* not on screening devices such as marital status. If comprehensive reform is impossible, means testing auxiliary benefits could be desirable. Certainly a "social adequacy" program assuring a basic level of support regardless of contributions is welcome.

CHANGING THE BENEFIT FORMULA

The benefit formula itself (described in detail in the appendix) could be changed. There are those who would like to see greater correspondence between benefits paid and creditable wages. (Currently there is a progressive tilt in the Social Security replacement rate; a very large fraction of the first small bit of average indexed monthly wages is replaced.) There are those who would alter the "bend points" in the formula—the points at which the additional benefits paid per dollar of additional average indexed monthly earnings are altered—in order to reduce the benefit payments at the upper and middle sections of the earnings scale. Gradually reducing the growth of these bend points is one way to bring the overall level of benefits under control.

But changing the bend points, which are used to calculate the primary insurance amount, merely adjusts the amount paid; it does nothing to alter the basic structure of benefit payments. For example, the spouse's benefit might be reduced by a reduction in the bend points, but the benefit would remain. Just dropping the upper bend points slightly would reduce the benefits paid to well-off future retirees, but there are not enough of these retirees for this to lower the deficit of the Social Security system significantly. In order to have a substantial impact on the long-run financial solvency of the system, the bend points would have to be lowered where substantial aggregate benefits are being paid.

The Reagan administration's original Social Security proposals provided for such a gradual lowering of the bend points in order to reduce benefit growth. But these proposals met heavy political opposition because there would be a sharp reduction in benefits for early retirees. This approach, however, could be combined with, for example, a restructuring of the benefits for families or spouses to ease Social Security's future financial burden.

RAISING THE AGE OF ELIGIBILITY

Because of the long-term financial solvency problems of Social Security, increased life expectancy, and changing patterns of retirement, various proposals have been put forward to increase the age of eligibility for full Social Security benefits. The 1983 Social Security Amendments provide for a gradual increase in the age of eligibility for full benefits from 65 to 66 at the turn of the century to 67 a couple of decades later. But this reform (the total effect of which amounts to a savings of between one fourth and one third of the OASDI deficit prior to the 1983 Amendments) will not even offset the increases in life expectancy over the next 70 years. Fortunately, the increases in retirement age are to be phased in gradually after a grace period so that no particular age group is severely discriminated against and individuals, firms, and private institutions have sufficient time to adapt.

Our definition of old age is outmoded. The fraction of the population reaching age 65 is much larger now than at any other time in our history, and a 65-year-old today may well live to 80 years of age or beyond. Future gains in life expectancy are predicted, although the rate of increase estimated by the Social Security Administration is slower than that estimated by the Society of Actuaries.

Given the trend to a longer life span, one sensible proposal might be to raise the retirement age gradually so as to keep a constant ratio of retirement life expectancy to potential working life over time. In short, as life expectancy increases, for whatever reason, so would the "normal" retirement age. This proposal could, by itself, eliminate the total pre-1983 Social Security Amendments deficit of 1.8 percent of taxable payroll. In contrast, the proposal to raise the age of eligibility for full benefits gradually to age 68 would only eliminate about two thirds of the pre-1983 deficit in OASDI, about 1.2 percent of taxable payroll.[5]

Two points should be kept in mind with respect to raising the age of eligibility for full retirement benefits. First, the amount of the increase and the period over which it is phased in will have substantially different effects on different generations. A rapid upward shift in the age of eligibility would provide greater immediate fiscal relief for the system at the expense of people soon to retire. The more gradually the program is phased in, the more distant the financial savings and the more the burden will be carried by younger persons.

Second, because there is enormous heterogeneity among the elderly with respect to life expectancy, current health status, income, and the physical demands of their jobs, any across-the-board increase in the age of eligibility for full retirement benefits would raise serious issues of equity. An individual with a physically demanding and dangerous job might have good cause to resent an increase in the "normal" retirement age to 68, whereas someone with a less physically taxing position, say, a college professor, probably would continue to work even after he became eligible for Social Security benefits.

Furthermore, the long-term cost saving of pushing back the age of eligibility for full retirement benefits might be counteracted by such features of the system as the early retirement option or the disability program. For example, a larger fraction of those who were due to retire at age 68 might start collecting disability benefits at age 62 or 65, thereby partially offsetting the savings of later retirement. And there would be added pressure on the disability program from an increased legitimate caseload. While increases in the age of eligibility for full retirement benefits could be structured to cure the Social Security system's retirement and disability deficit, the inequities mentioned above would require serious attention.

Where do these reform proposals leave us?[6] Each of them has something to recommend it, but *none* is a panacea, addressing as they do only some of Social Security's several problems. The taxation of benefits could contribute to the financial solvency of Social Security and reduce the excess benefits going to the wealthiest retirees, but it does not target payments to needs. While indexing at only a portion of the CPI increase could provide an enormous long-term reduction in benefit growth, it too would do nothing to reform the basic structure of the benefit formula.

On the other hand, means testing of the auxiliary benefits is probably a good idea. The original assumptions about dependency on which these benefits are based no longer hold today, and vast amounts are being paid out unnecessarily. Means testing the entire program, however, is undesirable. A means-tested component does make sense in a two-tier system.

Changing the bend points in the computation formula has much to recommend it. This can be done in such a way as to achieve simultaneously a reduction in future benefits (to bring the system into actuarial balance) *and* a restructuring of the benefits to alter replacement rates at different income levels. Such a change is also more flexible than the CPI adjustment in attempting to deal with the financial solvency of the Social Security system. Raising the age of eligibility for full retirement benefits could wipe out the deficit in OASDI, but because there is enormous heterogeneity among the elderly, it would also generate significant problems in terms of equity.

Taken together, these reform proposals could be very valuable. For example, combining changes in the bend points with increases in the age of eligibility for full retirement benefits, with the taxation of benefits, and with means testing of auxiliary benefits, would go a long way toward streamlining the benefits, targeting them to need, and setting Social Security back on a sound financial footing.

A TWO-TIER SYSTEM

Many problems in the Social Security system relate to the conflict between its twin goals of income adequacy and earned benefits. Most critics of the program propose reforming it in the direction of one goal or the other. Recommendations also have been put forward for a two-tier system—separating the transfer and annuity components of Social Security. But the measures thus far proposed usually do not fill the bill.

The most common two-tier approach, and the one that exists in some Western European economies, is to pay *everyone* a fixed amount per month (the transfer component) plus a second (annuity) benefit related to previous earnings. For example, each individual might receive $200 per month (an elderly couple would receive $400 per month) and, in addition, an earnings-related benefit. While such a system does provide an income guarantee and earnings-related benefits, it necessitates a huge expenditure of funds. Further, since the flat benefit goes to everyone, substantial outlays will be made to those who may not need them. Undoubtedly, this common minimal floor is an attempt to remove some "stigma" that may attach to receiving a means-tested benefit. But the failure to means test the transfer part of the program is simply outmoded; an enormous price is being paid to avoid whatever disgrace recipients might experience. It is unnecessary to have the flat transfer payment made to everyone; it is much more cost conscious and effective to pay it only to those who are in need of the funds.

In the United States, the Supplemental Security Income (SSI) program is an example of a means-tested transfer plan for those at the very bottom of the income scale. As is currently the case for the SSI program, the transfer portion of a two-tier Social Security system might be financed out of general revenues. General revenue financing would have one salutary effect: it would require the transfer portion of Social Security to compete *openly* with other government priorities—including tax cuts. It would push policymakers to consider the value of transfer payments to the elderly in relation to other social priorities and to promote cost-effective measures for making those transfer payments. It would also spur assessment of the differing needs of those in dissimilar circumstances (e.g., marital status) in order to operate the transfer program both efficiently and equitably.

In principle, the insurance part of a two-tier program—i.e., the earnings-related benefits—could operate according to any benefit formula desired. This portion of the system also could have a progressive benefit formula with successively smaller fractions of income replaced as preretirement earned income increases. The base against which earnings are calculated could be either some average indexed monthly earnings, some peak earnings, or cumulative lifetime earnings for taxable contributions. The choice among these will substantially affect the nature of the benefits and the perceived equity of the system. For example, assuming a separate, income-tested program to ensure the social adequacy of Social Security, it does not make much sense to have a progressive benefit formula based on short periods of covered earnings. It would be fairer, and most consistent with the compensation for imperfect annuities markets, to give everyone an *identical* return on their lifetime contributions. This would treat everyone equally in the earnings-related part of the system and thus eliminate the inequities that undermine support of the Social Security system. A more direct tie to cumulative lifetime contributions also would enable firms and employees to rationalize and plan *total* retirement income support (i.e., private pension programs plus Social Security).

In order to determine the changes in contributions and benefits that would be required to mold the current Social Security system into one that separates transfer and annuity programs, it is necessary to review some basics. In a situation where there is no Social Security system, the retirement income of the elderly comes from the savings they accumulated when they were working. If a Social Security system were introduced, it would collect taxes from those currently working and pay benefits to those currently retired. Those who are retired at the dawn of the Social Security system receive a huge transfer or windfall since they did not pay taxes when they were working. *All* of their benefits are transfer payments from the general working population. The same windfall occurs when there is an extension, expansion, or additional type of coverage (e.g., Medicare) provided by Social Security. Those who are already retired or are about to do so receive a pure transfer financed by those who are then working. Those who paid into the Social Security system during their working years expect to receive benefits when they retire. Those benefits, in turn, are paid by the workers in the succeeding generation.[7]

If Social Security tranfers were modest, there would be little cause for concern. The problem is that they are massive, that they are often capricious with respect to who gets them relative to who pays for them, and that they will continue for decades. Giving everyone an identical return on their cumulative lifetime contributions would create a situation where the expected present value of benefits equaled the expected present value of contributions (using the appropriate interest rate). But, because the current Social Security system has a massive long-term deficit, it may be necessary to credit an interest rate lower than the market rate or the rate of economic growth.

Ideally, though, everyone could and should receive an *identical* rate of return, which could be easily calculated and reported so that an individual would know what coverage to expect under different circumstances. This would eliminate the transfer payments in the earnings-related part of the system—by far the largest component of Social Security. Claims for special treatment or for transfer payments from the general population could *all* be adjudicated in a *separate* program where *need* would be the basis for determining extent.

The failure of our Social Security system to make this separation and to target income adequacy and earned benefits goals separately is a source of immense redistribution of income in our society—most of it unintended and much of it from those with less to those with more.

In the next several decades, trillions of dollars of transfer payments are due to be paid out. Positive transfer payments from the OASDI system will continue for decades, depending on income, marital status, etc. Even a modest reduction in these transfers could make a huge contribution to cutting the OASDI deficit as well as to the overall equity of the Social Security system.

Consider the elimination of the transfer payments as defined above—i.e., benefits in excess of contributions by employers and employees plus interest—*only* for those future retirees with average indexed monthly earnings above the mean. Table 6.2 shows that this minor policy change would save about $1.2 trillion in real (1984) present value benefits. (This proposal would not eliminate transfer payments to those already retired.)

Some components of the Social Security system, such as the progressive benefit formula, make a greater fraction of the benefits paid to the poor transfer payments. But because the actual dollar amounts paid by Social Security to rich and middle-income people are much larger than the actual dollar amounts paid to the poor, transfer payments made to the rich and middle class are actually greater.[8]

It would be hard to imagine Congress explicitly voting to transfer $1.2 trillion to well-off elderly individuals over the next several decades financed by a flat-rate payroll tax (with no exemptions or deductions) on the general population. Yet that is exactly what our current Social Security system does! Reforming the system to provide everyone an identical return on his lifetime contributions could be accomplished by separating the transfer and annuity functions. I believe that such a two-tier system is the most desirable structural reform available. It would not only put Social Security on a sound financial footing, but would accomplish this goal in a target-effective and cost-conscious manner.

Table 6.2
Simulation Results: Eliminating Transfers to Those with AIME above the Mean*

1. OASI System Totals, 1983-2057 (in trillions of 1983 dollars)

	Present Value Taxes	Present Value Benefits	Surplus/ Deficit (-)
Current Law	$10.3	$10.3	—
Eliminate Transfers	10.3	9.1	1.2**

2. Estimated Benefit Reduction by Age Group

Age (in 1984)	Reduction in Benefits by Eliminating Transfers to Those above Average AIME*** (in billions of 1983 dollars)
62 or more	125
52-61	283
42-51	195
32-41	159
less than 32	515

*   Excluding those already retired.

**   This amounts to two-thirds the pre-1983 deficit.

*** Rising life expectancies prevent still larger reductions for younger workers.

Source: Author's calculations.

WINNERS AND LOSERS

Each of the suggested reforms to reduce benefit growth and to make the Social Security system financially solvent over the next 75 years has different implications for the intergenerational distribution of benefits. As illustrated in Tables 6.1 and 6.2, the various types of Social Security reforms discussed above would have different effects on individuals depending on their ages. For example, eliminating the transfer payment for those who have average indexed monthly earnings above the mean would result in a substantial reduction in benefits for those above the mean who are not yet retired. Less than full indexing for the rise in consumer prices would have only a small impact on currently retired individuals and those soon to retire but a slightly greater impact on the retirement benefits of younger workers. If the CPI adjustment was CPI minus 2 percent beginning in 1985, the expected benefits of a retired family would be about 90 percent of what they are under current law, whereas those due to retire in three decades would have their benefits reduced by about 20 percent in real present value terms. Whereas a proportional CPI adjustment would tend to affect all those in a given age group to the same extent, a bend point adjustment could affect the progressivity of the benefit formula and hence the distribution of benefits *within* any age group. Increases in the age of eligibility for full retirement benefits will affect the ultimate benefit payouts to people of different ages differently.

Not only will structural reforms of the Social Security system have unequal effects on different age groups, but so will the anticipated surplus in OASDI expected to result from the 1983 Social Security Amendments. It was optimistically believed that the surplus due to accumulate in OASDI over the quarter century beginning in 1989 could be used to reduce the need for subsequent tax increases to finance Social Security benefits when the baby boomers retire. Historically, though, the accrual of surpluses was a signal to raise benefits or to provide new types of benefits.

Table 6.3 highlights the intergenerational problems and economic tradeoffs of resorting to pay-as-you-go financing during the years of a potential surplus. In panel A there is a description of what happens to the system and to different age groups when, to keep the Social Security program in balance year by year, a tax reduction accompanies the surplus. This situation would cause a substantial reduction in tax rates over the surplus years, reaching a low of 8.4 percent combined for employers and employees in the year 2007. These cumulative tax reductions would amount to about $668 billion and would redistribute huge sums across age groups. If we resorted to full pay-as-you-go financing, so that the surplus was just a prelude to an immediate across-the-board tax

Table 6.3
Simulation Results: The Intergenerational Politics and Economics of Resorting to Pay-as-You Go Financing During Years of Potential Surplus

A. Tax Cut to Deplete Surplus

System Totals

Tax rates hit a low of 8.4% in 2007 (compared to 11% currently legislated), rise above 11% by 2025, and reach 13.6% in mid-twenty-first century

Cumulative tax reduction approximately $668 billion, 1990-2024.

Tax reduction by age group (in billions of 1983 dollars)

62 or Over	52-61	42-51	32-41	32 or Under
—	9	39	105	222

B. Benefits Ratchet Upward to "Use" Surplus, Ultimately Paid for by Still Larger Tax Increase; Tax Rates Hit 20.2% in Mid-Century

System Totals, 1984-2058 (in trillions of 1983 dollars)

Taxes	10.3
Benefits	13.7
Deficits (if no subsequent tax increase)	3.4
Tax Increase	3.4

Net Transfer Change Relative to Current Law (in billions of 1983 dollars)

72 or Over	62 or Over	52-61	42-51	32-41
70	135	258	351	422

Source: Author's calculations. (Note: Ages refer to ages in 1984.)

N.B. Amoung those "32 and Under" (in 1984), those born beginning in the early 1980's have a lifetime net tax increase; those born beginning about 1996 do worse than under current law—eventually much worse.

rate cut as the surplus accrued, it is clear from the table that the primary beneficiaries would be those working at the time—i.e., people in their 20s and 30s.

However, in the more likely case of benefits ratcheting upward to consume the surplus and no subsequent tax increase, the deficit would be quite pronounced: $3.4 trillion. A tax increase in discounted 1983 dollars of that magnitude would be necessary to keep the system on a pay-as-you-go basis and balanced each year. Further, this deficit would have enormously different impacts on different age groups. While the increased benefits would be of only minor consequence to those now elderly, their effect would grow substantially through time. The net change in aggregate transfers (panel B) would be, for example, two-and-one-half to three times as large for those in their 40s as for those in their 60s.

CONCLUSION

The time has come to rethink what we are attempting to accomplish through Social Security. If our goal is to provide an efficient, equitable, and target-effective program, we must gradually tighten the link between benefits and cumulative contributions. This could be accomplished by separating the transfer and annuity components of the system. Further, phasing out transfer payments to those with incomes above certain levels could substantially reduce Social Security's long-term financial solvency problem.

Those who believe that the OASDI system is (and will continue) on a financially sound footing for the next 75 years are making extremely optimistic assumptions about demographics, economics, and politics. Increases in life expectancy may well exceed those forecast by the Social Security Administration; many have judged the fertility rates predicted by the Social Security Administration to be unrealistic;[9] and, perhaps most significant, it is not likely that the OASDI system will be able to accumulate an enormous surplus, collect interest, and use these funds to finance the Social Security benefits of the baby boom generation. Whatever surplus develops probably will be used either to reduce Social Security taxes, increase Social Security benefits, provide additional types of Social Security benefits, or aid the Hospital Insurance program.

The Social Security reforms discussed above offer various ways to reduce Social Security benefit growth, contain costs, and put the system on a sound financial footing.[10] We must evaluate these alternatives now, so that a consensus can be reached before it is too late. Separating the transfer and annuity functions, it seems to me, is the most sensible structural reform possible.

CHAPTER 7

Alternative Methods of Finance

INTRODUCTION

The pressing need for Social Security revenue has renewed debate over the best way to finance the system. Relying almost exclusively on pay-as-you-go financing through payroll tax collections has long been considered the most desirable approach in the United States. But elsewhere—for example in many European countries—it is common for general tax revenues to fund some of these benefits. A third option is to build a genuine trust fund. Each of these methods has its pros and cons.

PAYROLL TAX FINANCING

In the United States the popularity of payroll tax financing of Social Security benefits stems from the fact that such taxes make it *appear* that people are contributing to a fund that is designated explicitly for them when they retire. Actually, nothing could be further from the truth; their taxes pay for the Social Security benefits of current retirees.

There are compelling arguments for relying exclusively on payroll taxes to finance Social Security. First, the payroll tax is an efficient revenue device—a comprehensive flat tax levied without deductions and exemptions.[1] Second, the payroll tax is specifically earmarked for this program, which presumably precludes the use of this revenue for other purposes. Third, to the extent that individuals perceive their payroll tax contributions as a form of saving, the distortions these contributions otherwise would create in savings and labor supply would be partially mitigated, since the perceived net returns would not be reduced by the tax rate—it would be regarded as a saving deposit with a fair return.

But there are drawbacks to relying exclusively on payroll tax financing. For one thing, it is slightly regressive. In addition, it establishes a situation in which low- and middle-income workers are financing enormous transfer payments to well-off retired individuals. Further, in the long run, it probably will lead to a larger system than would be possible under alternative types of finance. Finally, there is a constant temptation to solve short-run financial problems by dipping into general revenues.

GENERAL REVENUE FINANCING

As an alternative, there are those who propose financing Social Security benefits through general tax revenues. After all, it is argued, the spending must be financed somehow. But a tax is still a tax. Shifting from payroll tax financing to general revenue financing would simply transfer the cost of Social Security to other parts of the budget; it does nothing to help reach a sensible balance between what we want and what we can afford. In addition, because of exemptions and deductions, the tax base that would be provided by the personal income tax would be smaller than the tax base provided by the payroll tax.

Joseph Pechman and others have argued that, because of the alleged regressivity of the payroll tax, general revenue financing would be more equitable.[2] But there are at least two flaws in this point of view. First, every dollar of government revenue does not have to be raised from progressive tax sources even if it is considered desirable for the tax side of the budget to be progressive. Second, and more significant, it is not only taxes but taxes and benefits taken as a whole that determine regressivity. Overall, Social Security benefits are extremely progressive, and therefore the combined taxes and benefits are too.

The best case that can be made for financing Social Security benefits out of general revenues is that it may force a closer examination of the nature and desirability of Social Security benefits—an argument advanced by many but most forcefully by Milton Friedman.[3] I am in sympathy with the idea that all items in the federal budget should compete for funds. Needs must be evaluated against resources. If there were a shift to general revenue financing *prior* to a reevaluation of the Social Security benefit structure, the result would be a larger, less efficient, and less effective social insurance program, as well as one we may not be able to afford.

In one of the compromises reached as part of the 1983 Social Security Amendments, Social Security will be removed from the budget of the United States government in 1993. This was the result of conservatives' fears that general revenue financing would lead to increased Social Security benefits and liberals' fears that Social Security could not successfully compete with other items—for example, defense spending—in the general budget.

FINANCING AND MARITAL STATUS

The issue of payroll tax contributions versus general revenue financing reopens the thorny question of the appropriate tax and benefit treatment of the individual versus the family.[4] Those whose work consists solely of household tasks do not pay Social Security taxes. Therefore, they receive no credit toward future

Social Security benefits. But if these individuals are married, they will qualify for the spouse's benefit. Thus, while Social Security benefits are paid, in a sense, on a family basis, taxes are levied on individuals. In some cases, a working spouse earning much lower wages than the primary earner in the family may get more Social Security benefits by collecting the spouse's benefit instead of his or her own. In this situation, the second wage earner would have paid in substantial taxes with *no incremental* return on their contributions.

Still other problems in terms of the equity of Social Security benefits are created by divorce and remarriage. Some homemakers fall through the cracks in coverage because they are not married for a sufficient length of time to collect the spouse's benefit. Others may accrue benefits from several spouses. There are several sensible alternatives that could begin to redress this problem. One, for example, is the earnings-sharing approach, which would split the earnings of the worker into two records so that the homemaker has a documented contribution credit history that he or she could carry with him or her in the event the family breaks up.

When taxes are levied on one basis and benefits paid on another, it is difficult to establish equity. It is sometimes argued that women receive a worse deal than men under Social Security. Certainly, there are inequities in the treatment of working versus nonworking women—specifically in cases where a working woman would receive greater Social Security benefits on the basis of the spouse's benefit than she would receive on the basis of her own earnings history. But then she also would be receiving transfers from the spouse's benefit above and beyond what she and her husband, and their employers, paid in.

The question of who receives a worse deal overall is not easily resolved. After all, the life expectancy of women substantially exceeds that of men so women will be paid for a much longer period of time. This has become a major issue in the insurance industry, and various options have been proposed to deal with it including charging different premiums for the same annuity or providing different annuities (but the same expected present value of benefits) for the same premium payment.

FINANCING AND RAISING TAXES

As a result of the Social Security Amendments of 1983, Social Security taxes are scheduled to reach a combined (employer and employee) 15.3 percent of payroll in 1990. If the surplus currently being projected does not accumulate and/or if the amounts exempted from income taxes are indexed to inflation, it will be necessary to raise payroll taxes again—and substantially—early in the next century to cover the OASDI deficit. Figure 7.1 illustrates how high OASDHI tax rates would go under alternative economic/demographic scenarios. Clearly, if nothing is done to reduce the growth of Social Security benefits from this point on, tax rates may reach prohibitive levels. Under the most pessimistic assumptions, a combined rate of 41 percent is envisioned. While there will undoubtedly be political resistance to the tax rate increases illustrated, the longer we wait to do something major about restructuring Social Security in a sensible manner, the more

Figure 7.1
Combined Employer-Employee Tax Rates Under Alternative Economic-Demographic Assumptions*

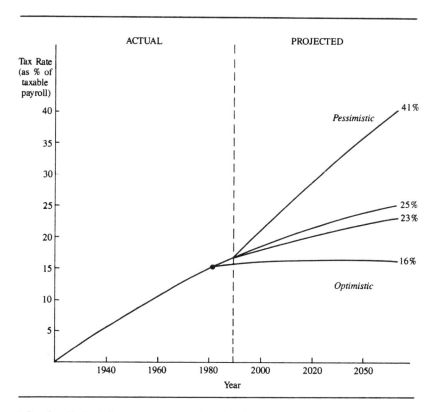

* Surplus dissipated or exempt amounts indexed.

difficult it will be to avoid them. The higher these tax increases, the fewer resources will be available to meet other public needs and private wants and the worse the distortions of the major economic decisions that are affected by Social Security taxes and benefits.

As shown in Table 7.1, most West European countries have much higher payroll tax rates than the United States. Whereas the combined OASDI payroll tax rate for 1981 in the United States was 10.7 percent, in Italy it was 24.5 percent and in the Netherlands it was 34.9 percent.

Table 7.1 also indicates that in many countries general revenue financing supplies a substantial fraction of total expenditures

Table 7.1
Comparative Payroll Tax Rates, 1977 and 1981, Proportion of General Revenue Financing for OASDI, Selected Advanced Economies

Country	Combined Payroll Rate, 1981	Proportion General Revenue Finance, 1977
Austria	21.1%	34.8%
Canada	3.6	N.A.
France	13.0	9.7
Germany	18.5	24.2
Italy	24.5	N.A.
Japan	10.6	N.A.
Netherlands	34.9	7.8
Sweden	21.2	18.9
Switzerland	9.4	14.8
United Kingdom	21.5*	N.A.
United States	10.7	0.8

* For all programs; separate data for OASDI not available.

N.A.: Not Available.

Source: U.S. Congress, Senate, Special Committee on Aging, *Social Security In Europe*, December 1981.

on OASDI. For example, general revenues cover about 8 percent of OASDI in the Netherlands, 10 percent in France, 15 percent in Switzerland, 19 percent in Sweden, 25 percent in Germany, and 35 percent in Austria. In the United States, general revenue financing of OASDI expenditures amounts to less than 1 percent. But we may be headed in the direction of these West European welfare states—tax rates so high they seriously erode work incentives and reliance on general revenue financing for a significant portion of Social Security outlays. I believe that we *can* have a humane and substantial social insurance system without such traumatic tax increases and such large use of general revenue financing.

BUILDING A SURPLUS

There are those who argue for complete privatization of Social Security and the building of a genuine trust fund.[5] Contributions would be invested in real capital, and benefits would be paid out of accumulated earnings and principal—similar to the operations of an insurance company. Clearly, there would be problems with this approach: the size of such a trust fund would be enormous (trillions of dollars eventually), the lack of actuarially fair annuity markets would present obstacles, and the current generation of taxpayers would be forced to pay twice—once for their own retirement and once for current retirees.

Still, there are substantial and sound reasons for building a surplus.[6] Building a surplus in Social Security, other things being equal (such as the government's budget being balanced), would increase *national* saving, provide more capital for the economy, and, ultimately, increase our standard of living. Of course, it could be argued that, if our purpose is to increase our rate of national savings, *there is no reason it must or should be done in the Social Security system.* We could, for example, run a surplus in general funds. Or, to be more realistic, we could substantially reduce the deficit.

Retiring some of the national debt would have major consequences in terms of long-run national saving, investment, productivity, and income levels. It would also substantially affect the intergenerational distribution of wealth. Our current fiscal policy of running very large deficits has led to the first increase in the ratio of national debt to gross national product since World War II. If continued, this will mean that future generations of Americans will inherit a larger debt and the burden of higher taxes to pay interest on that debt. Further, a growing fraction of our national debt is owned by foreigners, and thus interest payments will send money out of the country. The result is likely to be a decrease in the standard of living of future Americans compared to what it might have been had we run a balanced budget.

Building a surplus, on the other hand, in order to avoid the necessity of large tax increases on future generations—say, to fund Social Security benefits—will make our heirs doubly better off; they will have higher levels of income and lower tax burdens than otherwise. The desirability of shifting the burden of taxes onto current taxpayers in order to raise the standard of living for future generations of Americans clearly depends on *ethical* judgments about the intergenerational distribution of wealth, which depend on future rates of economic growth.

In the quarter century after World War II, the U.S. economy grew at a rate sufficient to make each generation almost twice as wealthy as the one that preceded it. At such growth rates, there would be no need for concern about leaving a large debt to much wealthier future generations. But for the past 15 years, there has been a substantial slowdown in the growth of productivity. At the very least, there is enormous uncertainty over whether we will be able to restore our productivity growth rate. If not, our children and grandchildren will be only moderately better off than we are. A continued slowdown in productivity growth dramatically changes the nature of the ballgame, leaving future generations with larger tax burdens. Thus, building a surplus in the Social Security fund has significant implications for future income levels and the intergenerational distribution of tax burdens.

Partly because it would be imprudent to assume productivity growth rates equivalent to those of the immediate post-World War II period and partly because it is not fair to pass the burden for our Social Security benefits onto future generations, I believe we must anticipate the enormous increase in Social Security expenditures that will occur in the 21st century. I believe that we should gradually build a surplus in the OASDI Trust Fund and *prevent* its dissipation for other purposes (such as general tax cuts, spending on other programs, etc.). This slow buildup would help reduce overall deficits and therefore the accumulation of debt we are leaving our heirs. It would also spread necessary tax rate increases over a larger span of time and shift some of the tax burdens to current taxpayers. If it turns out that productivity growth surges over a substantial span of time, we can reconsider the appropriateness of tax increases and benefit cuts.

Table 7.2 presents my calculations of the intergenerational distribution of tax burdens that will occur depending on how we choose to finance Social Security benefits. As can be seen, *hundreds of billions of dollars are at stake.* Assuming that benefits are kept at currently projected levels, pay-as-you-go financing is a much bet-

Table 7.2
Alternative Proposals and Examples of Shifting the Tax Burden and Benefits Across Generations

A. *Present discounted value of taxes and benefits projected under current law for OASI through 2057: approximately $10.3 trillion.*

B. *Examples of Intergenerational Redistribution of Tax Burdens and Benefits with different Financing/Benefit Assumptions: Aggregate Net Benefits minus Taxes, in discounted 1983 dollars (billions) for younger persons.*

Birth Year	Current Age	Current Law	Retirement at 68*	Pay-As-You-Go (no surplus used to smooth rates)
1943-1952	32-41	216	99	321
1953-1990	31 or less	1030	756	1252

* Phased in gradually through 1990.

Source: Author's calculations, based on updated simulation model described in M. Boskin, M. Avrin, and K. Cone, "Modelling Alternative Solutions to the Long-Run Social Security Funding Crisis," in M. Feldstein, ed., *Behavioral Simulation Methods in Tax Policy Analysis* (Chicago: University of Chicago Press, 1983).

N.B. Those born unitl the early 1980s pay lower lifetime taxes than under current law. Those born later pay much more. These results are not directly comparable to those from previous studies due to several factors: use of updated life tables, different discount rates; incorporation of 1983 amendments, etc.

ter deal for middle-aged people who will retire in the early part of the 21st century because it shifts part of the huge burden onto future generations. Building a substantial surplus, on the other hand, would, in effect, tax middle-aged people now to help provide for their own retirement.

Full funding of Social Security—that is, building a genuine trust fund—is neither practical, necessary, nor desirable. First, we presume that future generations will be wealthier. While we are unsure just *how much* wealthier they will be, they will be somewhat richer. Thus, forcing the current generation of workers to pay both for their own benefits and those of current retirees is unfair—at least part of that burden could and should be borne by future, wealthier generations. Second, the government has the power to tax. Thus, expected future tax revenues must be taken into account. It is only when the expected future benefits dramatically exceed expected future tax revenues that Social Security becomes financially insolvent and that benefits must be reduced and/or taxes raised. The trust fund reserve system of insurance companies is a sound basis for providing private individual care and security. The funds for expected benefit payouts to individuals come from current reserves, earnings on those reserves, and expected future premiums. Benefits are paid out to the very people who contributed. If an individual drops out of the system and stops paying premiums, he will not receive the benefits. But it is not necessary for Social Security to be run in this manner. The power to tax allows the government to shift benefits and taxes among people in a manner that private insurance could not.

Since the people paying Social Security taxes and those receiving Social Security benefits are usually separated by at least one generation, the question of building a surplus is principally one of intergenerational equity. We can no longer assume that our children and grandchildren will be able to afford, without major disruption, the substantial tax increases necessary to pay for the projected growth in Social Security benefits.

POLITICAL CONSIDERATIONS

We have never been able to run a substantial surplus in Social Security. As soon as it was realized that substantial revenues were accruing, we changed immediately from an insurance-type system to a pay-as-you-go system. But the fact that we have been unable to sustain a surplus in the past does not necessarily mean that we could not do so in the future. Previously, when Social Security surpluses accrued, they were used to increase benefits—usually across the board to the needy and wealthy alike—by the development of new types of benefits and/or by delaying projected tax increases. Still, there is a clear upper limit both to the extent that benefits can be financed by taxing more income or by increasing coverage. Eventually, *all* income will be taxed and *everyone* will be covered, and we will only be able to provide an implicit return equal to the sum of the rates of population and real productivity growth, at constant tax rates.

It is critical that we begin to accumulate a Social Security surplus in order to prevent major disruptions in the system in the 21st century. But it also is clear that there will be pressing demands for those funds. For example, the Hospital Insurance (HI) system will begin to run enormous deficits at just about the same time that OASDI begins to accumulate surpluses. The political temptation will be to allow HI to borrow from OASDI.[7] If this happens, then the financial solvency of the Social Security retirement and disability package evaporates. In essence, we would be back where we started—that is, having to raise taxes to cover OASDI. There also might be a temptation to use the projected Social Security surplus to finance the general government deficit. That is another reason why conservatives wanted to remove Social Security from the budget.

It will take remarkable political leadership and education to secure public support for a Social Security surplus, to restore confidence in the system, and to resist succumbing to the carnivorous appetites of those pushing other spending programs. I am cautiously optimistic that we will be able to do so, though our history on this matter provides little assurance.

If the surplus that is expected to accumulate is dissipated and/or reforms to slow the growth of benefits and place Social Security on a more sound long-term financial footing are ignored, the financial schism between generations will worsen. Taxes will be pushed onto future generations of workers. The national saving rate will decrease as the Trust Fund dissipates, resulting in less available capital to finance investment, to increase productivity, and to raise future standards of living.

When the baby boom generation retires, we will have a Social Security system that does not provide benefits to some who need them, that taxes people to provide benefits for which they have no need, and that imposes prohibitive payroll taxes on workers, lessening their incentive to work and report income. In addition, a large and growing fraction of the population will be dependent for a greater part of their lives on public income support because of the low level of their own private saving. At that time, hard-pressed workers will certainly resist tax rate increases of 5, 10, or 15 percentage points. The larger elderly population, meanwhile, will push for these tax increases to finance not only existing bene-fits, but also new ones. A confrontation between workers and retirees will arise (involving trillions of dollars) that will create the greatest polarization along economic lines in our society since the Civil War.

CONCLUSION

The alternatives to pay-as-you-go financing of the Social Security system are not very palatable. General revenue financing, for example, simply shifts the funding burden. Because of the differ-ences between a government and a private insurance program, full funding of Social Security is not the answer. There is no sound alternative to solving the funding problems of the Social Security system except to slow the growth of Social Security spending. If this is not done, a large, disruptive tax increase in the 21st century, which will create financial antagonism between the elderly and nonelderly generations of Americans, cannot be avoided.

There are sensible changes, however, that will allow us, at least partially, to mitigate this impending crisis. One is to allow the projected surplus in OASDI to accrue rather than to let it be dissipated by financing HI, other government spending pro-grams, or tax decreases. Building a surplus will help for two rea-sons: it will provide sorely needed increases in national savings (by decreasing the overall government deficit) and it will lessen the tax burden imposed on the next generation by the baby boomers' retirement.

How large a surplus to build and who should pay the taxes over what span of time are deeply ethical questions concerning the intergenerational distribution of wealth. In a rapidly growing economy, there would be less need to build a surplus so that the current generation of workers would partially pay for its own retirement income support. But can we really count on anything like the super-rapid productivity growth we experienced in the quarter century after World War II? Or is the more recent pro-ductivity slowdown more likely to be the norm for the next 20 or 30 years? No one has the answers to these questions. My own view is that we can expect modest, sustainable rates of productivity growth and should plan accordingly. This being the case, short of dramatic changes in demographics—such as much shorter life expectancies or much greater fertility rates—we have no choice but to deal with the financial problems of the Social Security system. It will be an extreme test of our political process to see if, as the Social Security surplus accumulates, we can resist the temptation to dissipate it on other programs or tax cuts.

CHAPTER 8

*Toward a Solution: A Two-Tier Social
Security System*

INTRODUCTION

The problems plaguing Social Security—its long-term funding difficulties, its inequities, and its adverse incentives—have a common solution: separating the transfer and annuity functions of the program. While Social Security benefit growth has been the prime ingredient in reducing the incidence of poverty among the elderly, transfers to the elderly poor should be financed from general revenues, not from payroll taxes. It makes little sense to finance an income guarantee for the aged poor from a tax that bears heavily on the working poor. Also, switching to general revenue financing, by requiring Social Security transfers to compete openly with other government priorities (including tax cuts), will force policymakers and the public to determine the value of transfers to the elderly in relation to other social priorities.

Those who can provide for themselves should be prevented from relying on transfers from society at large. The most obvious way to accomplish this is to *limit* the size of the Social Security program, leaving provision for old age beyond minimum, compulsory amounts to private saving and insurance plans. The scope of choices now open to workers, of course, can be *increased*.

In order to achieve this goal, I propose *tying Social Security benefits directly to contributions*. I would totally eliminate the progressivity of the benefit formula (allowing the transfer portion of the program to establish an adequate minimum for those at the bottom) and provide an actuarially *equivalent* return per dollar of contribution for each and every Social Security participant. *All* claims for special treatment and general income support would be handled through the transfer portion of the system, not the insurance portion. This would immediately eliminate a huge amount of inadvertent transfer payments from relatively poor taxpayers to relatively well-off retirees that results from the complex Social Security benefit formulas. The two-tier proposal will allow for *explicit* decisions regarding income redistribution rather than the current situation of redistributing tens of billions of dollars inadvertently.

While the two-tier system that I propose would be a major improvement in making our transfer payments more target-effective and cost-conscious and our social insurance programs much more efficient, it would not automatically eliminate the long-term funding problem. The gap between the present value of expected taxes and the present value of expected benefits would remain if everyone received an actuarially *fair* return. Somehow, society must come up with the difference, either in higher Social Security taxes, higher income taxes, or lower benefits. Virtually all proposals to restore solvency to the Social Security system involve benefit reductions. My proposal is simply to gradually restructure future benefits to levels compatible with currently legislated future tax receipts. We also need to tailor the specific types of coverage more directly to the needs of those involved.

HOW THE SYSTEM WOULD WORK

The two-tier Social Security system that I propose consists of a program of benefits tied tightly to taxes paid over one's lifetime (the first tier—Part A—or the annuity function) and a means-tested transfer payment program for those elderly individuals and families whose own resources are deemed insufficient (the second tier—Part B—or the transfer function). The overwhelming bulk of future elderly retirees would fall under Part A only. Part B, much like the current Supplemental Security Income (SSI) program, would supplement basic benefits (receivable under Part A) for low-income elderly individuals and families. The means test would be applied only *after* assignment of Part A benefits. It is my own preference that Part B be funded from general revenues and that the amounts and nature of the transfer payments compete openly with other claims on the public purse. A traditional argument against a means-tested Social Security system has been the concern that well under 100 percent of those who would be eligible would actually enroll in the program. This is apparently the case with Aid to Families with Dependent Children (AFDC), a means-tested program. However, the Social Security Administration will already have substantial information on the vast majority of those who might be eligible in the welfare part of the two-tier system. It can therefore simply request additional information from possible recipients if necessary and greatly reduce the number of eligible households who fail to enroll.

In Part A of the program, which would replace our primary current Social Security system, benefits received would be tied exactly to taxes paid. This would be accomplished through a system of accumulated credits—which would earn common, annually determined rates of return—for taxes paid. Thus, two individuals or families that paid the same taxes year by year would get the exact same benefits, irrespective of their other circumstances. To illustrate, suppose Mr. and Mrs. Smith pay $1,000 in Social Security taxes in 1985 and a like amount is paid on their behalf by their respective employers, for a total of $2,000. The $2,000 in contributions, while going into a Social Security Trust Fund and used to pay benefits for current retirees, would entitle the Smiths to credits for that year. These credits would receive an actuarially determined rate of return that is identical for *all contributions made* that year by each and every individual. If the Jones family had combined employer and employee contributions of $3,000, they would receive one-and-a-half times as many credits, each of which would receive the identical rate of return as those of the Smith family. Correspondingly, if the Wilson family had $1,000 of combined employer and employee contributions, they would receive only half as many credits as the Smith family, but each credit would get an identical return attributed to it.

As the years go by, a record of Social Security taxes paid by each individual and/or family and their employers will be maintained. For the Smith family, the record between 1985 and 1987 might look as follows:

Year	Sum of Employer/Employee Contributions	Actuarially Determined Real Rate of Return
1985	$2,000	2.7%
1986	2,100	2.7
1987	2,200	2.7

When an individual retires, the retirement benefit to which he is entitled equals the sum of his credits for each year at the corresponding year's rate of return. Part A of the plan would provide indexed annuities, similar to those under current law, once an individual retires. There would be no ex post facto adjustment of rates of return to contributions made unless an absolutely unprecedented economic situation required it.

I also favor—although this is not necessary for establishing the two-tier system—equal sharing of all credits received between husbands and wives, irrespective of the division of earnings between them. Thus, each spouse would receive *one half* of the *sum* of the credits based on the combined earnings of *both* spouses. This earnings-sharing approach would dramatically improve the equity and viability of our social insurance system—particularly with divorce and remarriage so common. If this earnings-sharing approach is adopted, then each *individual* would have a Social Security record, similar to the one illustrated above, based on half the combined earnings of the two spouses.

The rates of return would be chosen conservatively by actuarial projection to make certain that future Social Security taxes will be sufficient to cover projected benefits (barring extreme economic disruption or dramatic, rapid demographic changes). Since the rate of return would be set annually and could be revised upward or downward as appropriate, a downturn in the economy or major demographic change would have to be quite severe to cause disruption.

In addition to providing this mechanism to ensure a more secure financial future for Social Security, the two-tier system offers a more equitable approach to contributions and benefits. In the first place, one of the problems with the current system is that single people pay for survivors insurance, subsidize spouse's benefits, and so forth—a situation that is inefficient and unfair. A more direct targeting of Social Security contributions made to benefits received could be accomplished in Part A through a formula based on commonly accepted insurance principles. (For example, the contribution applied to survivors insurance would be based on actuarial principles and depend on age, number of dependents, and so forth.) Also, under Part A, the link between contributions and benefits would be tight and direct.

Second, the current Social Security system promises benefits based on a complicated formula related to an individual's average indexed monthly earnings. Because of Social Security's long-term financial solvency problems, periodic adjustments and changes in the laws, and changes in marital status, number of children, etc., the actual "defined-benefit" is very uncertain.

In contrast, taxes paid into Part A of my proposed Social Security system would share the advantages of contributions into a defined-contribution private pension plan—although there would be two differences. First, the return would be set conservatively, and thus somewhat below that available on private investments, but would be much less risky, thereby making retirement planning considerably less uncertain. Second, in the case of a private pension plan, the contributions made by an individual and/or his employer are invested—for example, in the stock market. The actual benefits payable at retirement depend on the performance of the investment. In Part A, however, there would be no investment of the proceeds. The Social Security system could still be financed on a pay-as-you-go basis (whereby current taxes are used to pay current benefits and future benefits are financed by taxes on the next generation). The desirability of building up a surplus—with a partial or complete trust fund—is therefore a completely separate issue from the desirability of switching to a defined-contribution plan. (At current tax rates, a surplus would accrue for about 30 years beginning in the 1990s if we do not index the exempt amounts in the income tax and if we have the political will to maintain a surplus.)

While it is true that the "rate of return" applied to contributions under Part A might be lower than the return on investing in private markets, it is not true that young workers would get a "bad deal" as a result. This is because the level of benefits for retirees is set by the rate of return applied to current taxes, and young workers must pay for the benefits of current retirees. If young workers were credited with a higher return, their taxes would have to be raised in order to finance the benefits of current retirees. Counting these higher (income or payroll) taxes, the rate of return would be less than that in my plan.

Third, for all those fully covered under the two-tier system, transfers (defined as the difference between the expected present value of benefits and taxes) will be virtually eliminated. If the proposed system were phased in gradually, with some people treated under the two-tier system and others treated under the existing system (for example those over a certain age), considerable transfer payments would be made for a while. But *eventually* they would be phased out, and we would be moving toward a system that would be much fairer, more efficient, and simpler.

The two-tier approach also offers the advantages of easy-to-comprehend annual financial reports that will facilitate both the administration of the program and personal financial planning. Figure 8.1 presents a typical reporting document that the new Social Security system could provide annually to each individual and family. This information could greatly facilitate each family's overall financial planning (including decisions on private saving and purchase of private insurance). It would cut through the morass of misinformation currently provided and the complexities of Social Security laws, treat everyone equally, and make the system easier to comprehend and administer. If the earnings-sharing approach that I favor—but which is a *separate* issue from acceptance of the basic two-tier structure of the proposed new

Figure 8.1
Sample Annual Social Security Contribution/Coverage Report—1986

Name:	William Smith
Social Security No.:	100-00-0001
Age:	40
Marital Status:	Married; 2 children

Total Social Security Taxes, 1985:	$ 1,500.00
Spouse's Taxes, 1985:	$500.00

Social Security Credit: One half of total of own plus spouse's taxes (1/2 x $2,000.00) =	$1,000.00

Expected Real Rate of Return on 1985 Taxes:	2.7%

Previous Taxes Credited, Accumulated at Each Year's Return, as of 1985:	$14,000.00

Annual Benefits Estimated at Retirement if Current Tax Level Continues:	$6,000.00

Survivor's Benefits: Coverage: wife & children
In event of death, based on history of taxes
through 1985:

Wife's benefit/year:	$3,500.00
Children's benefits (each)/year:	$2,000.00

Disability Benefit: Coverage: covered
In event of disability, based on history
of taxes through 1985:

Annual Benefit:	$7,500.00

Additional information and complete histories may be obtained by writing any Social Security office.

Social Security program—is adopted, then each adult worker in the household would get a similar report. Such individual reports would prove a decided advantage in ease of administration under this program.

The explicit information contained in these annual reports would greatly facilitate decisions on private saving and private insurance that could then supplement the modest funds provided by Part A of the two-tier Social Security system. In fact, changing to a two-tier Social Security system would increase incentives for private saving—for example, contributions to an enhanced individual retirement account (i.e., one with a greatly expanded maximum contribution).

If it is deemed desirable to rely on private saving more than we currently do and programs such as enhanced individual retirement accounts are adopted, the rate of return on contributions to Social Security could be adjusted downward so that future retirees rely more on their individual retirement account saving and somewhat less on their Part A Social Security benefit. In fact, I strongly favor such a move. Enhanced individual retirement accounts are often suggested as an *alternative* to Social Security—or at least to part of the contributions—for young workers. But this would not alter the fact that the retirement benefits of current retirees and those soon to retire are going to be financed by taxes on those currently working. Thus, if young workers were allowed to opt out completely—or even partially—from the Social Security system, income taxes would have to be increased to make up the difference.

Still another advantage of the two-tier Social Security system proposed here is that it would facilitate private saving. Under current law, the Social Security system is radically different from private saving in its use of marginal resources and thus does not contribute to real capital formation. This is so for two reasons. First, since Social Security is financed on a pay-as-you-go basis, it does not have funds to invest in capital markets and therefore does not generate increased capital formation and economic productivity. Second, because of the Social Security benefit formulas, the linkage between incremental contributions made and incremental benefits received at retirement is so weak and returns so uncertain that incremental contributions are viewed as taxes on labor earnings, not saving or insurance purchases.

In the two-tier plan I propose, incremental contributions paid to Part A would provide an actuarially identical return to each contributor in terms of his future benefits, as compared to the hodgepodge of uncertain returns expected under the current system. Thus, the labor market distortion of piling the payroll tax on top of the income tax would be reduced. Still, unless a surplus were generated—for example by raising taxes and/or by lowering the rate of return to allow for an accumulation of funds—no real capital formation would occur. But if a surplus does accrue—either under the current system or under my plan—Social Security (in the aggregate) would be adding to national saving in much the same way as expanded private saving would.

Thus, while under current law, the enormous expected growth of Social Security crowds out private saving and private insurance, the proposed two-tier system combines with private saving and private insurance in a much more direct, simpler, and efficient manner, facilitating private saving at the margin. I believe that we should rely more on private saving, although, for reasons discussed above, we cannot rely on it completely for retirement income support.

The two-tier system proposed here is not a panacea for all of Social Security's problems. But it would be simpler, fairer, and more efficient than the Social Security system under current law. It does not eliminate the long-term deficit problem, but it does provide a flexible mechanism for dealing with Social Security's long-term financial solvency and short-term cash flow problems in an equitable manner, rather than by periodic, unfair, quick-fix solutions. And, by insisting on identical treatment of all individuals and families, it attempts to eliminate haphazard and inequitable redistribution of hundreds of billions of dollars among those in the same generation and trillions of dollars across generations. Further, it facilitates personal financial planning for old age and encourages private saving at the margin.

FINANCIAL IMPLICATIONS OF ALTERNATIVE APPROACHES

Numerous recommendations have been made for solving the financial problems of Social Security and for addressing its various inequities and inefficiencies. The extent of Social Security's financial problem is illustrated in the 75-year, long-term actuarial projections for OASDI (explicitly excluding Hospital Insurance) shown in Table 8.1. The table presents taxes collected (including taxes paid by those who do not survive to retirement), expected

Table 8.1
Base Case Results (Under Current Law)*

I. Results by Age Group (in 1983 $billions, discounted to 1983)

Age-Group #	Birth Years	Retirement Starts	Taxes	Paid by Nonsurvivors	Benefits	Transfer in Absolute Dollars	Transfer as a Percent of Benefits
5	-1912	-1977	$339.7	$15.1	$3,117.8	$2,778.0	89.1
4	1913-22	1978-87	425.2	75.3	1,242.1	816.9	65.8
3	1923-32	1988-97	650.8	129.4	1,213.4	562.6	46.4
2	1933-42	1998-2008	793.2	167.3	1,213.7	420.5	34.6
1	1943-52	2009-18	1,174.2	272.5	1,390.3	216.1	15.5
X	1953-90	2019-57	4,391.4	983.6	5,421.3	1,029.9	19.0

II. Results Per Family (in 1983 $thousands, discounted to 1983)

5	-1912	-1977	$8,804	$77,598	88.6
4	1913-22	1978-87	25,303	70,458	64.1
3	1923-32	1988-97	43,566	79,321	45.1
2	1933-42	1998-2008	66,390	97,439	31.9
1	1943-52	2009-18	92,880	113,914	18.5
X	1953-90	2019-57	80,888	97,315	16.9

III. Total for System, 1983-2057 (in 1983 $billions, discounted to 1983)

TAXES: $10,313   BENEFITS: $10,310   SURPLUS: $2.9

Note: Discount rate for system and for individuals: 2.1 percent.

*As mentioned in chapter six, these simulation results and those that follow are not directly comparable to those of earlier studies discussed previously in this volume. Among the imperent differences between the current results and earlier studies are one or more of the following: the use of updated life expectancy tables which predict greater life expectancies for today's younger workers (thereby bettering their return relative to that computed with earlier life tables); incorporation of various features of the 1983 amendments; use of a more recent set of intermediate economic and demographic projections; and different discount rates. The studies discussed previously often come to many similar qualitative, but very different quantitative, conclusions. The major difference is the later date, and therefore younger age, at which social security becomes a bad deal.

benefits, and transfers (defined as the difference between the expected present value of benefits and taxes)—both in absolute dollars and as a percentage of benefits—for six groups of retirees: those born prior to 1913; 10-year age groups of those born between 1913 and 1922, 1923 and 1932, 1933 and 1942, 1943 and 1952; and a larger group of those born between 1953 and 1990. Corresponding data on a per family basis is presented in the second panel of the table. The third panel reports the total for the entire OASDI system over the 75-year period, 1983 to 2057. All projections use the Social Security Administration's intermediate assumptions.

As can be seen, the system is in actuarial balance, with $10 trillion of taxes expected to be collected and $10 trillion of benefits expected to be paid out over this 75-year horizon. Intergenerational transfers remain enormous but decline steadily as a percent of benefits for succeeding age groups. But, taking economic, demographic, and political forces into account, current projections suggest that the long-term deficit probably has not been eliminated by current law. Because of our likely inability to accrue large surpluses over the 1990–2020 period and/or our inability to tax increasing numbers of elderly persons on one half of their Social Security benefits, it is likely that a deficit of over $1 trillion will reemerge.

The next several tables report the projected results of alternative methods of dealing with Social Security's potential long-term $1 trillion deficit. Table 8.2, for example, illustrates the results of a program that eliminates transfers above and beyond contributions plus interest for those with average indexed monthly earnings (AIME) above the average for their age group. As compared to the base case, this program would reduce benefits by about $1.2 trillion, leaving the system (under current projections) with a surplus as large as the projected deficit under indexing or dissipation of the surplus. Hence, this program appears sufficient to achieve overall financial balance in the Social Security system over the 75 years under consideration.

Panel 1 of Table 8.2 shows that the taxes collected would be unchanged but the benefits would change dramatically. While those born prior to 1913 would be unaffected by this scenario, recent retirees and those soon to retire would lose about 10 percent of their benefits, and the transfer portion of their benefits would fall from 66 percent to 62 percent. Those due to retire in 1988 would face an even more drastic benefit reduction of about

25 percent, and the transfer portion of their benefits would be cut from 46.4 percent to slightly over 30 percent.

The last two columns illustrate the change this scenario would make in terms of the transfer portion of benefits to each age group and evaluate the transfer portion of benefits as a percentage of the base-case transfer. Because the amount of the transfer in the base case declines from age group 5 to age group 1, the change in transfers in this scenario—both in the aggregate amount and as a percentage of the base-case transfer—is not monotonic with age. In any event, the most radical cut in transfer payments (i.e., about half of the total transfer payments due to be paid out in the program) falls on those due to retire in 2019 or beyond; still, substantial reduction is achieved through cuts in transfer payments to those due to retire in the balance of this century. Turning to the results per family, the table shows that aggregate benefits per family, the transfer as a percentage of benefits, and the change in the transfer portion of benefits from the base case all follow a pattern similar to that for the aggregate for each age group. Those hit the hardest are those born between 1923 and 1932—i.e., those due to retire in the decade beginning in 1988—although the change in the transfer portion of benefits would be roughly uniform over age groups 1, 2, and 3.

Table 8.3 reports the results of the proposal to increase the age of eligibility for full retirement benefits to age 68, phasing in this change from 1985 to 1991. Recall that, under current law, a very gradual increase in the age of eligibility for full retirement benefits—first to age 66 and then to age 67—is scheduled to be phased in early in the next century. Thus, this proposal raises the age of full eligibility one more year and phases it in more quickly. Relative to the base-case results, panel 3 shows that, for the total system, benefits fall substantially, taxes rise slightly, and a surplus of about two thirds of a trillion dollars would occur—the amount needed to deal with *either* the inability to run a surplus from 1990 onward or indexing the income levels at which Social Security payments would be exempt from taxation (but not both).

Note the differences between this proposal and the one to eliminate transfers to those retirees with average indexed monthly earnings above the average for their age group (illustrated in Table 8.2) in terms of the distribution of benefit reductions. While the aggregate benefit reduction is substantially less in the case of postponing eligibility for full benefits than it is in the case of eliminating the transfers, more of the burden of bringing

Table 8.2
Elimination of Transfers for Those With AIME Above Mean AIME

I. Results by Age Group (in 1983 $billions, discounted to 1983)

Age-Group #	Birth Years	Retirement Starts	Taxes	Benefits	Transfer in Absolute Dollars	Transfer as a Percent of Benefits	Change in Transfer (from Base-Case)	Transfer as a Percent of Base-Case Transfer
5	-1912	-1977	*	*	*	*	*	*
4	1913-22	1978-87	*	$1,117.3	$692.1	61.9	-$124.8	.847
3	1923-32	1988-97	*	930.8	280.0	30.1	-282.6	.498
2	1933-42	1998-2008	*	1,018.4	225.2	22.1	-195.3	.536
1	1943-52	2009-18	*	1,231.2	57.0	4.6	-159.1	.264
X	1953-90	2019-57	*	4,906.4	515.0	10.5	-515.0	.500

II. Results Per Family (in 1983 $thousands, discounted to 1983)

5	-1912	*	*	*	*	*
4	1978-87	$60,719	$35,416	58.3	-$9,739	.784
3	1988-97	55,674	12,108	21.8	-23,647	.339
2	1998-2008	77,711	11,322	14.6	-19,727	.365
1	2009-18	95,545	2,665	2.8	-18,369	.127

III. Total For System (in 1983 $billions, discounted to 1983)

TAXES: $10,313   BENEFITS: $9,132   SURPLUS: $1,181

Note: Discount rate for system and for individuals: 2.1 percent. The "change in transfer (from base case)" column indicates the contribution of each age group to changes in the system's surplus. Thus, if this scenario is implemented in a year when one of the age groups begins to retire, results for system finances may be readily calculated *except* that group X's contribution is only $419 billion by 2057 (the rest of its contribution comes after 2057).

* Same as base case. See Table 8.1.

Table 8.3
Raising the Age of Eligibility for Full Retirement Benefits to Age 68
(Phased in from 1985 to 1991)

I. *Results by Age Group (in 1983 $billions, discounted to 1983)*

Age-Group #	Birth Years	Retirement Starts	Taxes	Paid by Non-survivors	Benefits	Transfer in Absolute Dollars	Transfer as a Percent of Benefits	Change in Transfer (from Base-Case)	Transfer as a Percent of Base-Case Transfer
5	-1912	-1977	*	*	*	*	*	*	*
4	1913-22	1978-90	$425.7	$81.1	$1,189.4	$763.7	64.2	-$53.2	.935
3	1923-32	1991-2000	661.2	178.1	1,050.5	389.3	37.1	-173.3	.692
2	1933-42	2001-10	814.1	199.3	1,067.7	253.6	23.8	-166.9	.603
1	1943-52	2011-20	1,151.6	344.6	1,250.4	98.8	7.9	-117.3	.457
X	1953-90	2021-58	4,371.2	1092.8	5,127.3	756.0	14.7	-273.9	.734

II. Results Per Family (in 1983 $thousands, discounted to 1983)

5	-1912	-1977	*	*	*	*		
4	1913-22	1978-90	$26,003	$68,305	$42,302	61.9	-$2,853	.937
3	1923-32	1991-2000	51,544	73,349	24,805	33.8	-950	.694
2	1933-42	2001-10	76,711	94,699	17,988	19.0	-13,061	.579
1	1943-52	2011-20	101,265	110,920	9,655	8.7	-11,379	.459
X	1953-90	2021-58	82,567	94,046	11,478	12.2	-4,949	.699

III. Total For System (in 1983 $billions, discounted to 1983)

TAXES: $10,482   BENEFITS: $9,809   SURPLUS: $673

Note: Discount rate for system and for individuals: 2.1 percent.

* Same as base case. See Table 8.1.

Table 8.4
Results if Benefits Are Increased When Surplus Accrues

Age-Group #	Birth Years	Retirement Starts	Taxes	Paid by Non-survivors	Benefits	Transfer in Absolute Dollars	Transfer as a Percent of Benefits	Change in Transfer (from Base-Case)	Transfer as a Percent of Base-Case Transfer
I. Results by Age Group (in 1983 $billions, discounted to 1983)									
5	-1912	-1977	*	*	$3,187.7	$2,848.0	89.3	+$70.0	1.025
4	1913-22	1978-87	*	*	1,377.5	952.3	69.1	+135.4	1.166
3	1923-32	1988-97	*	*	1,471.8	821.0	55.8	+258.4	1.459
2	1933-42	1998-2008	*	*	1,564.7	771.5	49.3	+351.0	1.835
1	1943-52	2009-18	*	*	1,820.4	646.2	35.5	+430.1	2.990
X	1953-90	2019-57	*	*	8,100.2	3,708.8	45.8	+2,678.9	3.601

II. Results Per Family (in 1983 $thousands, discounted to 1983)

5	-1912	*	$79,861	$71,057	89.0	+$2,263	1.033
4	1913-22	*	78,135	52,832	67.6	+7,677	1.170
3	1923-32	*	96,326	52,760	54.8	+17,005	1.476
2	1933-42	*	125,785	59,395	47.2	+28,346	1.913
1	1943-52	*	149,159	56,279	37.7	+35,245	2.676
X	1953-90	*	145,164	64,276	44.3	+47,849	3.913

III. Total For System, 1983-2057 (in 1983 $billions, discounted to 1983)

TAXES: $10,313   BENEFITS: $13,679   SURPLUS: -$3,365

Note: Discount rate for system and for individuals: 2.1 percent. Benefits reach a ratio of 1.309 times currently legislated levels in 2009 and remain at that ratio thereafter.

* Same as base case. See Table 8.1.

balance to the Social Security system is placed on those due to retire between now and 2021—i.e., when the baby boomers retire.

Table 8.4 illustrates what will happen if we follow our traditional pattern of raising benefits when the Social Security system begins to run a surplus in 1990. (Remember that, starting in 1990, OASDI is expected to run substantial surpluses for 30 years.) If those surpluses are not maintained to reduce the need for future tax increases to cover the benefits paid to the baby boomers but are used instead to increase current benefits, benefit levels will rise substantially. Once the benefits are increased, it will be very difficult to reduce them, even though, from about 2020 on, when the baby boomers start to retire and the number of people receiving Social Security benefits will rise dramatically, taxes will be insufficient to cover the benefits. The result will be a huge deficit or tax increases.

As compared to the current law, base-case scenario, the total benefits in this scenario will increase by over $3 trillion. The current (probably optimistic) projection of a system in actuarial balance will turn into a projection of a deficit of over $3 trillion—roughly twice the deficit prior to the 1993 Amendments! Since the surpluses are scheduled to accrue starting in 1990, those retiring from that year onward will receive substantial increases in benefits. Benefits ratchet up, so that, as compared to the current law, base-case projections, successive age groups of retirees receive larger and larger benefits. Compare, for example, those retiring in 1988, who will receive an average of $17,000 more per family, with those retiring in 1998, who will receive $28,000 more per family. The portion of benefits received as a transfer also would increase with successive age groups. For example, in the aggregate, the early baby boomers will receive $430 billion more in benefits, all of it transfer from younger taxpayers, and transfers would be almost three times as large as those expected under current law, base-case projections. Clearly, this would be a political disaster because, although taxes are not scheduled to change under this scenario, enormous pressure would be placed on the system to raise taxes.

In order to show the extent of this pressure, Table 8.5 illustrates what would happen if the deficits that would result from the above scenario were financed by pay-as-you-go tax increases. If benefits ratchet up during the years of surplus—the 1990–2020 period—and *remain higher,* we will start running substantial deficits around 2020. Table 8.5 presents the results of raising OASDI tax rates gradually to 20.2 percent in 2058. With 30 percent higher taxes, this would bring the system back into actuarial balance with total system benefits at almost $14 trillion as opposed to slightly over $10 trillion. Note that, while those born prior to 1933 would receive the same treatment as in the previous scenario, those born thereafter would not. Those born from 1943 to 1952 would come out almost the same, but those born from 1953 to 1990—the peak of the baby boom and subsequent period—will have similar benefits but a decrease in their aggregate transfers by over $1 trillion (since their taxes increase by $1 trillion). In short, this pay-as-you-go system shifts a huge part of the burden to those who retire from 2010 onward. For those born after 1990, transfers would shift from a negative $3.4 trillion (to make up the deficit) to a negative $2.3 trillion because those born between 1953 and 1990 would have paid an additional $1.1 trillion in taxes.

Table 8.6 illustrates what will happen if we adhere strictly to the principle of pay-as-you-go financing. By definition, the pure pay-as-you-go system is in long-run actuarial balance. Benefits would increase from 1990 o 2020 during the time of surplus, but then be reduced to come back into line with taxes. Over the 75-year projection period, taxes and benefits would balance at around the $10 trillion level. But the distribution of taxes and benefits by age group differs radically from the base case and the scenarios presented in Tables 8.4 and 8.5, in which the benefits permanently ratched up.

Comparing Tables 8.5 and 8.6 shows how the *timing* of projected tax increases or benefit reductions will affect various age groups in our society. For example, those yet to retire will receive far smaller benefits under strict pay-as-you-go financing than under benefit market—ranging from $260 billion less for those born between 1923 and 1932 to $2.5 trillion less for those born between 1953 and 1990. Taxes will be $100 billion higher for those born between 1923 and 1932 but fall $200 billion or so for those born between 1953 and 1990. For those born between 1943 and 1952, the results per family show $36,000 less in benefits and $9,000 less in taxes. Clearly, hundreds of billions, even trillions of dollars are at stake in the decision about whether to accrue a surplus or dissipate it.

Table 8.7 summarizes the results of these various alternatives for dealing with Social Security's long-term financial problems. As

Table 8.5
Results if Benefit Increases Are Financed by Pay-As-You-Go Tax Increases

I. Results by Age Group (in 1983 $billions, discounted to 1983)

Age-Group #	Birth Years	Retirement Starts	Paid by Taxes	Non-survivors	Benefits	Transfer in Absolute Dollars	Transfer as a Percent of Benefits	Change in Transfer (from Base-Case)	Transfer as a Per-cent of Base-Case Transfer
5	-1912	-1977	†	†	†	†	†	†	†
4	1913-22	1978-87	†	†	†	†	†	†	†
3	1923-32	1988-97	†	†	†	†	†	†	†
2	1933-42	1998-2008	$793.3	$167.3	$1,564.7	$771.4	49.3	+$350.9	1.835
1	1943-52	2009-18	1,182.8	272.8	1,820.4	637.6	35.0	+421.5	2.950
X	1953-90	2019-57	5,398.3	1,143.1	8,100.2	2,701.7	33.4	+1,671.8	2.623*

II. Results Per Family (in 1983 $thousands, discounted to 1983)

5	-1912	-1977	†	†	†	†	†	†
4	1913-22	1978-87	†	†	†	†	†	†
3	1923-32	1988-97	†	†	†	†	†	†
2	1933-42	1998-2008	$66,390	$125,785	$59,355	47.2	+$28,346	1.913
1	1943-52	2009-18	93,344	149,159	55,815	37.4	+34,781	2.654
X	1953-90	2019-57	99,609	145,164	45,556	31.4	+29,129	2.773*

III. Total For System, 1983-2057 (in 1983 $billions, discounted to 1983)

TAXES: $13,679   BENEFITS: $13,679   SURPLUS: $0

Note: Discount rate for system and for individuals: 2.1 percent. Tax rates rise from 10.98 percent in 2009 to 13 percent in 2018, 18 percent in 2032, and 20.2 percent in 2057.

*Those born after 1996 are worse off than in base case.

† Same as previous scenario. See Table 8.4.

Table 8.6
Results for Strict Adherence to Pay-As-You-Go Financing

I. Results by Age Group (in 1983 $billions, discounted to 1983)

Age-Group #	Birth Years	Retirement Starts	Taxes Paid	Paid by Non-survivors	Benefits	Transfer in Absolute Dollars	Transfer as a Percent of Benefits	Change in Transfer (from Base-Case)	Transfer as a Percent of Base-Case Transfer
5	-1912	-1977	*	*	*	*	*	*	*
4	1913-22	1978-87	$425.2	$75.3	*	$816.9	65.8	-$0.001	1.000
3	1923-32	1988-97	641.6	128.8	*	571.8	47.1	+9.2	1.016
2	1933-42	1998-2008	754.4	162.9	*	459.3	37.8	+38.8	1.092
1	1943-52	2009-18	1,069.2	256.8	*	321.1	23.1	+105.0	1.486
X	1953-90	2019-57	4,169.4	907.8	*	125.2	23.1	+222.1	1.216†

II. Results Per Family (in 1983 $thousands, discounted to 1983)

			*	*	*	*	*	*
5	-1912	-1977	*	*	*	*	*	*
4	1913-22	1978-87	$25,313	*	$45,146	64.1	-$10	.998
3	1923-32	1988-97	42,972	*	36,348	45.8	+593	1.017
2	1933-42	1998-2008	63,063	*	34,375	35.3	+3,326	1.107
1	1943-52	2009-18	84,829	*	29,086	25.5	+8,052	1.383
X	1953-90	2019-57	76,837	*	20,479	21.0	+4,052	1.247†

III. Total For System, 1983-2057 (in 1983 $billions, discounted to 1983)

TAXES: $10,310   BENEFITS: $10,310   SURPLUS: $0

Notes: Discount rate for system and for individuals: 2.1 percent. Only those born in 1982 and after are worse off under this scenario, because only in 2025 and after do tax rates rise above levels currently legislated.

* Same as base case. See Table 8.1.

†Those born after 1982 are worse off than in base case.

Table 8.7
System Finances, All Cases, 1983-2057

(in 1983 $billions, discounted to 1983)

	Taxes	Benefits	Surplus
Base Case	$10,313	$10,310	$2.9
Eliminate Transfers for Those with AIME above Mean	10,313	9,132	1,181
Raising the Age of Eligibility for Full Retirement Benefits to Age 68	10,482	9,809	673
Increase Benefits when Surplus Accrues	10,313	13,679	-3,365
Benefit Increases Financed by Pay-As-You-Go Tax Increases	13,679	13,679	0
Strict Adherence to Pay-As-You-Go Financing	10,310	10,310	0

can be seen, the outcome ranges from near balance in several cases, to a surplus (in the cases of raising the age of eligibility for full retirement benefits and eliminating transfers), to an enormous deficit (in the case of increasing benefits when a surplus accrues). As significant as these results are in the aggregate, what must be kept in kind is the impact that making these reforms would have on different generations of Americans. As indicated, choosing one approach over another can result in the reallocation of as much as a trillion dollars from one group of retirees to another—an amount that dwarfs the redistribution accomplished by tax policy changes that receive much more attention.

REDISTRIBUTION OF WEALTH UNDER
SOCIAL SECURITY

Even assuming that the Social Security system will be in actuarial balance for the next 75 years, unless reforms are enacted, there will remain another serious problem: the enormous, haphazard, and inequitable redistribution of income and wealth both among and within generations of Americans. This occurs because, under current law, Social Security benefits and taxes are not closely linked. Tables 8.8 and 8.9 illustrate the problem by comparing the rates of return and amount of transfer payments received by couples with various earnings in two different age groups: those born in 1953 and retiring at age 66, and those born in 1981 and retiring at age 67.

First, consider the pattern of rates of return, which clearly reflects the vagaries of the current benefit formulas. When the wife's level of earnings remains the same but the husband's earnings increase, the rate of return declines rapidly; conversely, when the husband's wages remain the same but the wife's earnings increase, the rate of return also declines substantially. This is true at all earnings levels.

Consider also the discrepancy in rates of return for two-earner versus one-earner couples. For example, compare two couples with spouses born in 1953 and with roughly equivalent incomes, one of which is a two-earner couple and the other a one-earner couple. In the first instance, let's say that the wife, on average, earns $9,000 and the husband $12,000, for a combined family taxable income of $21,000. In the second instance, the husband earns $20,000 and the wife nothing. In the latter case, total Social Security taxes will be slightly less, since the husband's earnings are slightly less than the combined husband/wife income of the first couple. The two-earner household gets a rate of return of 2.45 percent per year (see Table 8.8), whereas the one-earner household gets a rate of return of 3.24 percent per year. Translated into dollars discounted to the age of 65, the two-earner couple expects to get back a transfer slightly under $24,000, whereas the one-earner household gets a transfer of almost $89,000. Thus, the current system offers vastly different returns to couples with roughly the same income—depending on whether the household contains one or two wage-earners.

To take another example, this time in a higher income bracket, a two-earner family with a husband and wife earning $31,500 and $20,000, respectively, can expect to receive a rate of return of slightly over 1 percent and a transfer of −$129,000 (they get an expected present value of taxes *greater* than the expected present value of benefits)! Another couple with a husband earning $31,500 and a wife who does not work can expect a rate of return of 2.42 percent (about the same as that received by the two-earner, lower income household) but transfers of about

Table 8.8
Rates of Return and Transfers for Persons Born in 1953, Retiring at Age 66 (Various Family Situations)

Wife's Earnings	Husband's Earnings					
	$12,000		$20,000		$31,500	
	Rate of Return	Transfer	Rate of Return	Transfer	Rate of Return	Transfer
0*	3.75%	$84,703	3.24%	$88,580	2.42%	$30,542
$9,000	2.45%	$23,931	2.17%	$6,021	1.54%	-$59,818
$20,000	1.89%	-$19,528	1.58%	-$58,172	1.08%	-$128,988

Note: Real earnings are assumed to rise as in the SSA Trustees IIB intermediate assumptions. Transfers discounted to age sixty-five, in $1983.

* Does not work.

Table 8.9
Rates of Return and Transfers for Persons Born in 1981, Retiring at Age 67 (Various Family Situations)

Wife's Earnings	Husband's Earnings					
	$12,000		$20,000		$31,500	
	Rate of Return	Transfer	Rate of Return	Transfer	Rate of Return	Transfer
0*	3.56%	$119,597	3.05%	$117,737	2.18%	$12,566
$9,000	2.29%	$20,834	2.00%	-$14,425	1.35%	-$131,519
$20,000	1.75%	-$53,679	1.43%	-$120,307	0.90%	-$245,319

Note: Real earnings are assumed to rise as in the SSA IIB intermediate assumptions. Transfers discounted to age sixty-five, in $1983.

* Does not work.

$31,000—over $6,000 more than the two-earner, lower income household that earns about 50 percent less, and $160,000 more than the two-earner, higher income household. This redistribution of resources does not make any sense.

Table 8.9 presents corresponding data for those born in 1981. A similar pattern emerges, but the rates of return tend to be slightly smaller—varying from 0.9 percent to 3.6 percent per year—and the transfer is much smaller—from $120,000 to −$245,000—(except for low-wage husbands with nonworking wives) than for those born in 1953.

These are vast sums compared to the lifetime resources of these families. One or two hundred thousand dollars amounts to decades of tax payments for most families. Yet our Social Security system redistributes these sums—sometimes from the poor to the rich—without so much as a murmur from the public. Despite the fact that the overwhelming bulk of redistribution of funds in our society goes on through our Social Security system—both across and among generations—there is almost no *explicit* consideration of the desirability of such redistribution when reform is discussed. It is difficult to conceive of Congress passing a change in the income tax law that would cause even a modest fraction of this redistribution of the tax burden. Would it not be better to have the redistribution explicitly debated and approved by Congress?

The two-tier Social Security system that I recommend would eliminate the redistribution of wealth through Social Security unless explicitly reauthorized by Congress. It sets equal treatment as the norm, not as an accidental occurrence. Benefits and taxes would be tightly linked so that every individual receives a *common, identical* rate of return on his contributions. The system would be brought into financial balance by adjusting this rate of return.

To illustrate how this would work, let us take, as a base case, a common rate of return that can be applied to contributions under current projections without any increase in taxes or aggregate benefit reduction— i.e., under the assumption that the system is in actuarial balance. My calculations yield an estimated rate of return of 2.72 percent per year. Since this return is *identical* for everyone, every entry in tables corresponding to Tables 8.8 and 8.9 would have 2.72 percent as the rate of return and 0 as the transfer.

If the aggregate funding projections turn again to deficit— either because of economic or demographic changes or because our political process does not allow for accrual of the projected surplus—there is a simple mechanism for adjusting the system to financial solvency in such a way that everyone bears a fair, proportionate burden. All that would be necessary is a proportionate reduction in the rate of return. If, for example, we needed to come up with $1.2 trillion, the rate of return would have to be reduced from 2.72 percent to 2.4 percent per year. In this way, every individual would still be getting an identical return on his contributions. While there are numerous ways to adjust the rate of return so as to keep the system in long-term actuarial balance, I recommend annual adjustments in conjunction with the kind of reports received by participants in private pensions. Still, a variety of alternatives are available, such as adjusting the age of eligibility for full retirement benefits, providing higher rates of return to those at the very bottom of the income scale, and so forth.

Since we have a Social Security system in place, the question of transition arises. We cannot achieve a two-tier system overnight, nor should we. That would be unfair to people who planned their retirement based on very different rules and expectations. But various vehicles exist to facilitate the transition. For example, everyone above a certain age could be treated under the current system, which would be financed partly out of continued Social Security taxes from younger workers and partly out of general revenues. Or the system could be phased in gradually—say, over a 10-year period. In this case, everyone above a certain age would be exempted from inclusion in this plan, the next 10-year age group would be phased in 10 percent per year over 10 years, and thereafter everyone would be covered under the new plan. While this transition would be somewhat complicated, the public would be better informed about their future Social Security benefits than they are now (which would greatly increase the efficiency with which individuals purchase private insurance and save for retirement to supplement Social Security). And, after a few years, when the new system was fully phased in, everyone would be treated identically and equitably.

CONCLUSION

Our Social Security system is our most important and most expensive domestic program other than defense. It has been responsible for an impressive reduction in the incidence of poverty among the elderly, and it has provided types of insurance that private markets do not seem willing or able to provide (e.g., indexed annuities). But it suffers from severe problems—namely adverse work and saving incentives, capricious redistribution of hundreds of billions of dollars within generations and trillions of dollars from one generation to another, and potential long-run insolvency. Even if we have the political will to accrue the vast surpluses projected under current law without dissipating them on other programs (for example, on Hospital Insurance) or increasing benefits (which would totally destabilize the financial solvency of the system), we will still be saddled with an inefficient and inequitable social insurance program for the indefinite future. Nor is it clear that the current projections of actuarial balance are reliable. In my opinion, it would be imprudent to count on them.

As it is currently set up, our Social Security system is almost certain to lurch from crisis to crisis. Its long-term financial solvency is in doubt, and short-term, cash flow problems may arise due to recessions. It is inordinately complicated, providing very little information to those attempting to plan for their retirement. It is inefficient because it reduces work and saving incentives, and it is poorly targeted as a redistribution or insurance device.

Some reformers argue that the answer is to eliminate social insurance altogether. They contend that the Social Security system should be completely privatized, leaving individuals to provide for their own old age by relying on private markets. But because of the problem of adverse selection of risk, private markets are unlikely to provide actuarially fair annuities. Further, we would still need a welfare system for the indigent elderly and for those who had not, or could not, adequately prepare for their old age.

I reject both extremes of naive continuance of the current Social Security system or drastic movement toward privatization. What we need is a continued social insurance program but one tailored much more closely to what we can afford and one that contains the types of insurance we need—a program that is fairer, simpler, and more efficient than the current system. The best hope, as I see it, is the two-tier system proposed here.

The advantages of the two-tier system are many. Once through the transition, the two-tier system will be much simpler and fairer than our present Social Security program. The capricious redistribution of funds that occurs, sometimes from the poor to the rich, will be sharply reduced if not eliminated. Much more precise information will be provided, facilitating private planning for retirement. People will get what they pay for and pay for what they need. Labor market distortions caused by high marginal tax rates on earnings would be sharply decreased since many workers would view payroll taxes as saving at the margin. Finally, excess transfers projected under current law would be eliminated and long-term financial problems solved via adjustments in the rate of return.

Gradually phasing in the two-tier system after a grace period can minimize transition problems and will not yank the rug out from those who have already planned for their retirement or who are retired already. But, the longer we wait to begin to implement such a system, the less flexibility we will have in dealing with Social Security's potential long-run insolvency and the longer we will perpetuate an inefficient and inequitable program.

The best time to deal with the crisis looming in the future is now—before we reach the precipice. If we do not make structural changes in Social Security soon, our options will be sharply limited, our ability to respond to crises without major disruption will decrease, and the opportunity to set a sound future course for our most significant social program will rapidly slip away as the baby boom generation approaches retirement.

The History and Nature of Social Security Benefits

Social Security coverage has been extended to the point where about 90 percent of jobs are now included in the system. In order to draw the basic benefits, however, certain minimum requirements must be met; these typically take the form of having worked for a certain number of calendar-year quarters in the aggregate or in the recent past.

The following three fundamental steps are required to calculate an individual's Social Security benefit:

1. Calculation of average monthly earnings in covered employment (AME)—more recently, average indexed monthly earnings (AIME).
2. Calculation of an individual's primary insurance amount (PIA)—the basic Social Security benefit—from AME.
3. Calculation of an individual's benefits from PIA. In many cases, the benefit entitlement is exactly the PIA; in others, it is some fraction or multiple thereof.

Calculation of an individual's average monthly earnings in covered employment is less than straightforward. Rather than adding up an individual's wages and dividing by the number of months, as implied, a variety of exceptions and additions have, over the years, been put into the formula. For example, beginning in the mid-1950s, up to five years of an individual's earnings history might be excluded from the calculation, presumably the quarters in years of lowest earnings. Beginning in 1979, rather than adding up an individual's wages, wage histories were indexed by a formula that represented the growth in average wages in the economy. The indexing formula with which an individual calculated average monthly wages is entirely separate from the postretirement indexing of benefit levels for increases in the consumer price index. As wages rose more rapidly than prices on average (representing productivity growth), indexing wage histories by wage growth meant real increases in average monthly wages.

Once the average monthly wages are computed, a "piecewise linear" function of average monthly wages is used to compute the primary insurance amount (PIA)—the basic Social Security benefit. The original PIA was to be ½ of 1 percent of the first $3,000, plus 1/12 of 1 percent of the next $42,000, plus 1/24 of 1 percent of the next $84,000 of *cumulative* or lifetime creditable wages. But this provision in the 1935 law, which was much closer to an insurance analogy than the formulas that replaced it, was *never enacted.*

In 1939, a formula was put into force that was much more generous to persons then retiring; it was based not on cumulative lifetime contributions but on average monthly wages. It provided a primary insurance amount of 40 percent of the first $50 of average monthly wages, plus 10 percent of the next $200 (which was increased by 1 percent for each year with at least $200 of creditable wages). This style of benefit formula has been repeated ever since, with a progressive tilt in the "replacement rate." That is, a very large fraction of the first small bit of average monthly wages is replaced, with a declining fraction thereafter (although the formulas are now so complex that there can be an occasional modest upward lift for a small portion in the midsection of the range). Thus, the 1977 legislation provided 170 percent of the first $110 as the initial component of the PIA formula (for those reaching age 62 before 1979).

Figure A.1, panel A, illustrates the nature of the benefit formula. It is progressive in the sense that a higher ratio of PIA to AIME occurs for lower income workers. Thus, the benefit formula is an example of how Social Security's twin goals of earned entitlements and social adequacy clash head on and result in a compromise.

Table A.1 presents some major changes in Social Security provisions. Panel A describes extensions of coverage by type of employment; panel B describes changes in the benefit computation; panel C describes changes in the calculation of the primary insurance amount; panel D describes changes in the earnings test; and panel E describes changes in benefit types (especially the auxiliary benefits added to Social Security).

As can be seen from these panels, larger and larger fractions of the population progressively came under compulsory Social Security coverage, so that now all but a small percentage of the American labor force is included; the benefit computation became more progressive in the sense that some low-income years are now excluded and indexing is done using wages rather than prices. Some minor movements toward longer work history requirements are not detailed here. The PIA formula also substantially increased benefits in real terms, and virtually all of the increases were across the board—including large adjustments for benefits for well-off retired persons. The earnings test has been progressively liberalized, lowering the age of those exempt from 75 (in 1950) to 70 (by 1981) and raising the amount that can be earned without reduction of benefits. In addition, the implicit

Figure A.1

A. Primary Insurance Amount (PIA) and Average Indexed Monthly Earnings (AIME), 1983

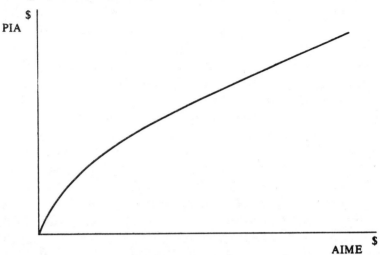

B. Growth of Social Security Benefits (OASDHI) in 1981 Dollars

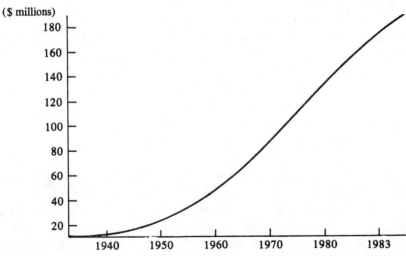

Source: U.S. Social Security Administration, *Social Security Bulletin, Annual Statistical Supplement,* 1982.

"tax" on earnings was reduced from 100 percent (a reduction of a dollar in benefits for every dollar earned beyond the exempt amount) to 50 percent.

Table A.1 also reveals the extension of benefit coverage. Beginning in 1956, women as young as age 62 could begin receiving

Table A.1
Some Major Changes in Social Security

A. Extension of Coverage by Type of Employment

Year	Extension
1950	Farm and domestic workers
1954	Farm self-employed
1956	Uniformed services
1965	Interns: self-employed physicians
1967	Ministers not under vows of poverty
1982	Federal employees in HI
1983	Nonprofit organizations; federal employees hired after January 1, 1984

B. Changes in Calculation of Benefits

Year	Change
1935	One-half of 1 percent of first $3,000 + one-twelfth of 1 percent of next $42,000 + one-twenty-fourth of 1 percent of next $84,000 of cumulative creditable wages. *Never implemented*
1939	40 percent of first $50 of AME + 10 percent of next $200 (increases by 1 percent for each year with at least $200 of creditable wages)
1954	Up to four years may be excluded
1956	Five years excludable
1975	Benefits indexed by CPI increase
1977	Wages indexed by average wage growth

Table A.1 (*continued*)

C. Changes in PIA Formula to Increase Benefits *

Date Effective	Benefit Increase (since last increase)	Increase in CPI	Benefit Increase minus CPI Increases
September 1950	77%	75.5%	+ 1.5%
September 1952	15	9.3	+ 5.7
September 1954	13	0.5	+12.5
January 1959	7	7.9	-0.9
January 1965	7	7.9	-0.9
February 1968	13	9.3	+ 3.7
January 1970	15	10.8	+ 4.2
January 1971	10	5.2	+ 4.8
September 1972	20	5.9	+14.1
June 1974–June 1982 Cumulative:	80.6	87.0**	-6.4**

* All increases except those for 1950-54 were uniform across the board.

** The CPI overstated inflation—both for the elderly and the general population—in this period by about 11 percent. (See M. Boskin and M. Hurd, "Indexing Social Security Benefits: A Separate Price Index for the Elderly?" *Public Finance Quarterly*, 1986.)

D. Changes in the Earnings Test

Year	Exempt Age	Exempt Amount (Annual Earnings)	Reduction
1950	75	$ 600	$1 for each $1 earnings
1954	72	1,200	1 month for each $80 in fraction
1981	70	6,600	$1 for each $2 of earnings (began in 1960)

Table A.1 (*continued*)

E. Changes in Benefit Types (Coverages)

---

1. Retirement

Year	Eligibility
1935	Retired Workers 65 and over
1956	Women aged 62-64 (actuarial reduction)
1961	Men aged 62-64 (early retirement with actuarial reduction)
2005-2022	Gradual rise to age 67, effective in 2022

---

2. Disability

| 1956 | Disabled worker aged 50-64 |
| 1960 | Under age 50 |

---

3. Dependents

1939	Wife over 65, 50 percent of PIA
1950	Under age 65 if caring for dependent child, 50 percent
1956	Aged 62-64 with actuarial reduction

---

4. Children

| 1939 | Under 18, 50 percent PIA |
| 1965 | 18-21 full-time student |

---

5. Divorced Wife

1965	Aged 65, married 20 years, dependent 62-64 with actuarial reduction
1972	Maximum eliminated; dependency requirement dropped
1977	Married ten years

Table A.1 (*concluded*)

---

6. Widows

	1972	100% PIA

---

7. Medicare

	1965	Age 65 or older entitled to benefits under Social Security or railroad retirement for HI.
	1980	Home health services with no restrictions

Source: Social Security Bulletin, Annual Statistical Supplement, 1982.

retirement benefits, although reduced by five ninths of a percentage point for each month under the age of 65; a corresponding provision, sometimes called the "early retirement" option, was instituted for men in 1961. The 1983 amendments will phase in—over the years 2000 to 2005, at two months per year—an increase in the age of eligibility from 65 to 66, with a corresponding gradual one-year increase between the years 2017 and 2022. Disabled workers age 50 to 64 became eligible for disability benefits in 1956, and those under 50 became eligible for disability benefits in 1960.

Benefits for dependents also have been progressively liberalized and "improved" from the initial arrangement in 1939. At that time, if the wife of a retired worker was over 65, she got 50 percent of the PIA in addition to the husband's PIA; if the child of a deceased worker was under the age of 18, he received 50 percent of his parent's PIA. By 1950, wives could receive reduced benefits at age 62. While in 1965, a woman who had been divorced had to be at least age 65, married for 20 years, and dependent to be eligible for full benefits (reduced benefits were available at age 62), by 1972 the dependency requirement was eliminated, and by 1977 the required years of marriage were reduced to 10 in order to provide some protection for women

Table A.2
Social Security Taxes - Examples of Growth

Year	Maximum Taxable Earnings	Contribution Rate from Employer and from Employee
1937	$ 3,000	1 %
1969	7,800	4.8
1983	35,700	6.7
1990*	Automatic Inflation Increase	7.65
2030†	Optimistic Assumptions	9
	Intermediate Assumptions	14
	Pessimistic Assumptions	24

* Scheduled.

† Projected, assuming non-accumulation of surplus from earlier years.

Sources: U.S. Social Security Administration, *Social Security Bulletin, Annual Statistical Supplement,* 1982. Projections from *1983 Annual Report* of the Social Security Administration Trustees.

who, because they had worked in the home rather than in the market, had not accrued their own earnings credit.

In 1965, Medicare was introduced for those over age 65. At that time, coverage for in-patient hospital services was limited to 90 days with various other deductible, coinsurance, and related provisions. Coverage for podiatry was added in 1972 and for home health care and related services in 1980. With Social Security benefits growing so much in the aggregate (see Figure A.1, panel B), the annual maximum taxable earnings and the tax rate applicable to those earnings have risen substantially. Some examples of these increases are presented in Table A.2.

Notes

CHAPTER 1

1. This estimate is based on an overall federal budget to GNP ratio of 20 percent. See Marcy Avrin in Michael Boskin, ed., *The Federal Budget* (San Francisco: ICS Press, 1982).

2. A social security system may also provide opportunities to increase the efficiency of the economy under certain conditions. For example, see R. Merton, "On the Role of Social Security as a Means for Efficient Risk-Bearing in an Economy Where Human Capital is Not Tradeable," in Z. Bodie and J. Shoven, eds., *Financial Aspects of the U.S. Pension System* (Chicago: University of Chicago Press, 1983); P. A. Samuelson, "Optimum Social Security in a Life-Cycle Growth Model," *International Economic* Review, Oct. 1975; and M. Feldstein, "The Optimal Level of Social Security Benefits," National Bureau of Economic Research, Working Paper No. 970, August, 1982.

3. See U.S. Social Security Administration, *Annual Report of Board of Trustees*, 1983. Also see Committee for Economic Development, "Social Security: From Crisis to Crisis?" (New York: CED, February 1984).

4. Michael Hurd and I attribute the overwhelming bulk of the decline in the labor force participation of the elderly from the late 1960s through the mid- and late 1970s to the sharp increase in the real level of Social Security benefits. See "The Effect of Social Security on Retirement in the Early 1970s," *Quarterly Journal of Economics*, November 1984.

5. Martin Feldstein in "Social Security, Induced Retirement and Aggregate Capital Formation" (*Journal of Political Economy*, 1974) and Alicia Munnell in *The Effect of Social Security on Personal Saving* (Cambridge: Mass.: Ballinger, 1974) launched the controversial argument that increased Social Security benefits decreased private saving for retirement.

6. The Social Security Administration (SSA) must forecast future revenues and outlays, deficits or surpluses. These depend on the growth rate of the economy, the number of workers and retirees, and other economic and demographic considerations. Since these cannot be predicted precisely, the SSA develops three "scenarios" called optimistic, intermediate, and pessimistic. Each scenario makes specific assumptions about future economic and demographic trends. For example, the optimistic scenario assumes (relatively) high rates of fertility and economic growth and low rates of inflation and unemployment; the pessimistic scenario makes assumptions at the other end of the spectrum. The *net* impact of economic and demographic trends on the financial solvency of the system is reflected in the labeling of the scenarios.

7. The provision of actuarially equivalent returns to all contributors should be distinguished from the concept of building a large surplus or fully funding the system. The two-tier proposal made here is compatible with any degree of funding deemed desirable.

8. The proposal to separate the transfer and annuity portions of our public retirement system is discussed and quantitative estimates provided in Michael Boskin, Marcy Avrin, and Ken Cone, "Modelling Alternative Solutions to the Long-Run Social Security Funding Problem," *Behavioral Simulation Methods in Tax Policy*, ed. Martin Feldstein (Chicago: University of Chicago Press, 1983). Previous Advisory Councils on Social Security also have suggested some movement in this direction.

CHAPTER 2

1. .See John Shoven and Michael Hurd, "The Economic Status of the El derly," in *Financial Aspects of the U.S. Pension System*, ed. Z. Bodie and John

Shoven (Chicago: University of Chicago Press, 1983). For details on incomes and relative incomes see M. Boskin, L. Kotlikoff, and M. Knetter, "Changes in the Age Distribution of Income in the U.S., 1968–84," NBER Working Paper No. 1766, Oct. 1985.

2. See U.S. Bureau of the Census, "Estimates of Poverty Including Noncash Benefits, 1979–91," Technical Paper No. 51, 1984. For a discussion of who fell through the safety net—heavily concentrated among widows—see M. Boskin and J. Shoven, "Poverty among the Elderly" NBER Working Paper in press.

3. Important contributions to the growing literature on concepts and measures of the economic well-being of the elderly include J. Schultz et al., *Providing Adequate Retirement Income* (Waltham, Mass.: Brandeis University Press, 1974); W. Kip Viscusi, *Welfare of the Elderly* (New York: John Wiley & Sons, 1979); M. Moon, *The Measurement of Economic Welfare* (New York: Academic Press, 1977); R. Clark et al., *Inflation and the Economic Well-Being of the Elderly*, (Baltimore: Johns Hopkins Press, 1984); and S. Danziger et al., "Implication of the Relative Status of the Elderly for Transfer Policy," in *Retirement and Economic Behavior*, ed. H. Aaron and G. Burtless (Washington D.C.: Brookings Institution, 1984).

4. Data from the Social Security Administration's Continuous Work History Sample suggest that the peak year of earnings occurred three to five years prior to retirement. A. Fox, in "Earnings Replacement Rates and Total Income: Findings From the Retirement History Study," *Social Security Bulletin*, October 1982, presents some adjustments (similar in spirit to those I make here) for taxes and career average earnings, and he comes to similar conclusions. He does not make the adjustments for the costs of children or for risk. Also, his excellent analysis presents replacement rates only as of 1976. For more on replacement rates see M. Boskin and J. Shoven, "Concepts and Measures of Earnings Replacement during Retirement," NBER Working Paper No. 1360.

5. The U.S. Bureau of Labor Statistics (BLS) develops equivalence scales to compare the income needed for different household types to have the same command over goods and services. In his *Providing Adequate Retirement Income*, Schultz reports several studies using BLS data. The range of estimates is from 51 percent as much income for a couple with the household head aged 35 to 54 and with two children aged 6 and 15, to 86 percent as much for a couple aged 55 to 64 without children. Taking account of taxes, Peter Henley estimates 80 percent and 70 percent maintain a lower income level and a higher income level, respectively. See Peter Henley, "Recent Trends in Retirement Benefits Related to Earnings," *Monthly Labor Review*, 1972.

6. For 10 years beginning in 1969, the Longitudinal Retirement History Survey followed over 10,000 households with spouses aged 58 to 63 and recorded information on labor force participation, marital and health status, assets, income sources, etc. Briefly, earnings are adjusted for taxes, based on historical income and payroll tax rates, and taxes are applied to taxable income in the numerator of the replacement rates for taxable income sources. The adjustment for costs of raising children is based on data from E. Lazear and R. Michael, "The Allocation Time and Income within the Household," unpublished manuscript, 1984. For a middle-income household with two children, roughly 20 percent of lifetime resources are devoted to expenditures on children. The rise adjustment analyzes earnings histories to examine the variance in earnings around its life-cycle trend and calculates the equivalent certain income based on estimates of what economists call the coefficient of relative risk aversion of two. See K. Arrow, *Essays on the Theory of Risk-Bearing* (Amsterdam: North-Holland, 1970).

7. M. Boskin, M. Avrin, and K. Cone, "Modelling Alternative Solutions to the Long-Run Social Security Funding Crisis," in *Behavioral Simulation Methods in Tax Policy Analysis*, ed. M. Feldstein (Chicago: University of Chicago Press, 1983).

8. J. Shoven and M. Hurd, "The Economic Status of the Elderly"; A. Pelle-chio, "Individual Gains and Losses Under the 1983 Amendments," mimeo, 1983.

9. Schultz, et al., *Providing Adequate Retirement Income.*

10. Victor Fuchs, "Though Much Is Taken," National Bureau of Economic Research, Working Paper No. 1269, January 1984.

CHAPTER 3

1. See U.S. Bureau of the Census, Special Studies, Series P-23, No. 128, September 1983.

2. Michael Boskin, M. Avrin, and K. Cone, "Modelling Alternative Solutions to the Long-Run Social Security Funding Crisis," in *Behavioral Simulations Methods in Tax Policy Analysis,* ed. M. Feldstein (Chicago: University of Chicago Press, 1983).

3. At one extreme, Martin S. Feldstein argues that Social Security has more or less replaced private saving dollar for dollar and that, in its absence, individuals would have approximately saved enough to receive the current level of benefits from asset income as opposed to Social Security. See Martin S. Feldstein, "Social Security, Individual Retirement, and Aggregate Capital Accumulation," *Journal of Political Economy* 82 (September-October 1974), pp. 905–26. At the other extreme, Robert J. Barro argues that this effect is entirely offset by adjustments in bequests and, hence, Social Security has not succeeded in transferring income from the younger generation to the older generation. See Robert J. Barro, "Are Government Bonds Net Wealth?" *Journal of Political Economy* 84 (November-December 1974), pp. 1095–1117. Empirical information on such intrafamily transfers, and the statistical evidence supporting alternative views on the effects of Social Security, private pensions, and other policies on private saving, retirement patterns, and the pattern of intrafamily transfers, is hardly conclusive but will be discussed in more detail in the chapters that follow.

4. Michael Hurd and Michael J. Boskin, "The Effect of Social Security on Retirement in the Early 1970s," *The Quarterly Journal of Economics,* November 1984, pp. 767–90.

5. E. Meier and C. Dittmar, "Varieties of Retirement Ages, President's Commission on Pension Policy, Nov. 1979.

6. Hurd and Boskin, "The Effect of Social Security on Retirement in the Early 1970s."

7. Ibid.

8. Ibid.

9. Social Security also could alter the labor supply of younger workers; see Richard V. Burkhauser and John A. Turner, "A Time Series Analysis on Social Security and Its Effect on the Market Work of Men at Younger Ages," *Journal of Political Economy,* August 1978. Several recent studies of retirement have concluded that Social Security has induced earlier retirement. See Michael J. Boskin, "Social Security and Retirement Decisions," *Economic Inquiry* 15 (January 1977), pp. 1–25; Michael J. Boskin and Michael Hurd, "The Effect of Social Security on Early Retirement," *Journal of Public Economics* (December 1978), pp. 361–77; Joseph F. Quinn, "Microeconomic Determinants of Early Retirement: A Cross-Sectional View of White Married Men," *Journal of Human Resources* 12 (Summer 1977), pp. 329–46; and Richard V. Burkhauser, "The Early Acceptance of Social Security: An Asset Maximization Approach," *Industrial and Labour Relations* (July 1980), pp. 484–92. Roger H. Gordon and Alan S. Blinder argue that effects net out. See Roger H. Gordon and Alan S. Blinder, "Market Wages, Reservation Wages and Retirement," National Bureau of Economic Research, Working Paper No. 513, July 1980. A skeptical literature review may be found in H. J. Aaron, *Economic Effects of Social Security* (Washington, D.C.: Brookings Institution, 1982). There was also a substantial earlier literature, mostly based on interviews with elderly retirees or time series or cross-section data as opposed to the panel data emphasized in recent studies. For example, Peter O. Steiner and Robert Dorfman, who estimate that only about 15 percent of elderly men would be considered to be out of the labor force for a lack of ability to work [*The Economic Status of the Aged* (Berkeley: University of California Press, 1957)].

CHAPTER 4

1. One need only examine the benefits and enrollments in disability in most Western European societies to realize that *some* disability is publicly financed early retirement.

2. Martin Feldstein, "Social Security, Induced Retirement and Aggregate Capital Accumulation," *Journal of Political Economy*, 1974; A. Munnell, *The Effect of Social Security on Personal Saving* (Cambridge, Mass.: Ballinger, 1974).

3. Robert Barro, "Are Government Bonds Net Wealth?" *Journal of Political Economy*, 1974.

4. For example, his argument assumes that nondistortionary taxes are available but existing tax devices distort, among other things, saving and labor supply decisions.

5. Michael Boskin, "Is Heavy Taxation of Capital Desirable?" U.S. Congress, Joint Economic Committee, Hearings, 1977.

6. Martin Feldstein, "The Effect of Social Security on Saving," NBER Working Paper No. 334, 1979.

7. Feldstein, "The Effect of Social Security on Saving."

8. A. Sen, "Isolation, Assurance and the Social Rate of Discount," *Quarterly Journal of Economics*, 1967; S. Marglin, "The Social Rate of Discount and the Optimal Rate of Investment," *Quarterly Journal of Economics*, 1963.

9. Feldstein, "Social Security, Induced Retirement and Aggregate Capital Accumulation."

10. D. Leimer and S. Lesnoy, "Social Security and Private Savings: New Time Series Evidence," *Journal of Political Economy* 90 (June 1982), pp. 606–42.

11. Martin Feldstein, "The Welfare Costs of Health Insurance," *Journal of Political Economy*, 1980.

12. See H. Aaron, "Economic Effects of Social Security" (Washington, D.C.: Brookings Institution, 1982) for a more complete bibliography and a somewhat different interpretation.

13. Feldstein, "Social Security, Induced Retirement and Aggregate Capital Accumulation"; V. Fuchs, *Who Shall Live?* (New York: Basic Books, 1974); and A. Enthoven and P. Drury, "Competition and Health Care Costs," in *The Economy in the 1980's*, ed. Michael Boskin (San Francisco: ICS Press, 1980).

14. If the discounted present value of each household's total contribution at retirement (for those already retired) or expected contributions including a correction for survival probabilities (for those not retired), labeled PVC^i, is compared with the expected retirement benefits similarly discounted and adjusted at the age of retirement, labeled PVB^i, an actuarially fair system can be defined as one where $PVC^i = PVB^i$. The expected present value of the transfers received by the participant $T^i = PVB^i - PVC^i$. For the overwhelming bulk of households already retired and due to retire in the near future, the transfers are positive.

Eventually, they become negative as the Social Security systems mature and the realities of the demographic situation take over (see Table 4.1).

CHAPTER 5

1. See M. Derthick, *Policy Making for Social Security* (Washington, D.C.: Brookings Institution, 1979).

2. One reason for the piecemeal extension of coverage was the traditional employer-employee withholding tax, which was not considered administratively practical for some occupations until recently.

3. See U.S. Senate, Special Committee on Aging, "Older Americans and the Federal Budget: Past, Present and Future," April 1984.

4. P. Ferrara, *Social Security Reform: The Family Plan* (Washington, D.C.: Heritage Foundation, 1982).

5. See L. Kotlikoff and D. Smith, *Pensions in the American Economy* (New York: National Bureau of Economic Research, 1983).

6. This is one of the reasons for my proposal to provide information analogous to that provided by private pension plans.

CHAPTER 6

1. See National Commission on Social Security Reform, "Actuarial Costs Estimates for OASDI and HI and for Various Possible Changes in OASDI," Washington, D.C., 1982.

2. See the U.S. Social Security Administration, *Social Security Bulletin, Annual Statistical Supplement*, 1982.

3. See Michael Boskin and Michael Hurd, "Indexing Social Security: A Separate Price Index for the Elderly?" *Public Finance Quarterly*, October 1985, and Bridges and J. Hambor, "The New CPI and Cost of Living Increases for OASDI and SSI," *Social Security Bulletin*, August 1982.

4. R. Ricardo-Campbell, "Social Security Reform: A Mature System in an Aging Society," in *To Promote Prosperity*, ed. J. Moore (Stanford, Calif.: Hoover Institution Press, 1984).

5. See National Commission on Social Security Reform, "Actuarial Costs Estimates for OASDI and HI."

6. Many other specific proposals have been made. A sample list would include changes in the treatment of divorced persons; eliminating the earnings test; providing earnings sharing for the credits in a marriage where only one person is working; eliminating the auxiliary benefits for early retirement cases; increasing the delayed retirement credit for years of postponed retirement past the first age of full eligibility; and changing the computation formula for determining the average indexed monthly earnings from age 62 to 65. Many of these proposals have desirable features.

7. The present value of each household's total contribution at retirement—PVC^i_R—can be calculated as

$$PVC^i_R = \sum_{t=1}^{R} C^i_t(1 + r)^{R-t}$$

where R is a given retirement age and r is the interest rate "credited" to a Social Security "account." All projected benefits are calculated so that they are the anticipated dollar amount times the probability of the individual surviving beyond age 65. The estimates are conditional on survival to retirement.

The expected retirement benefits at age of retirement—PVB^i_R—can be calculated as

$$PVB^i_R = \sum_{t=1}^{N} B^i_t(1 + r)^{R-t}$$

where N is 100, beyond which the survival probability is taken to be zero. Given that survival probabilities are already embedded in Bi and C, an actuarially fair system would be one where $PVC^i_R = PVB^i_R$. The expected present value of any transfer received by the participant would be defined as $T^i_R = PVB^i_R - PVC^i_R$.

8. See Michael Boskin, M. Avrin, and K. Cone, "Modelling Alternative Solutions to the Long-Term Social Security Funding Problem," in *Behavioral Simulation Methods in Tax Policy*, ed. M. Feldstein (Chicago: University of Chicago Press, 1983); and Michael Hurd and John Shoven, "The Distributional Impact of Social Security" in *Pensions, Labor, and Individual Choice*, ed. D. Wise (Chicago: University of Chicago Press, 1985).

9. Ricardo-Campbell, "Social Security Reform: A Mature System in an Aging Society."

10. See National Commission on Social Security Reform, "Actuarial Cost Estimates for OASDI and HI," for a discussion of other combinations of reforms.

CHAPTER 7

1. See R. Hall and A. Rabushka, *Low Tax, Simple Tax, Flat Tax* (New York: McGraw-Hill, 1982).

2. J. Pechman, H. Aaron, and M. Taussig, *Perspectives on Social Security* (Washington, D.C.: Brookings Institution, 1967); J. Pechman, "The Social Security System: An Overview," in *The Crisis in Social Security*, ed. Michael Boskin (San Francisco: Institute for Contemporary Studies, 1977); J. Pechman, *Federal Tax Policy*, 4th ed. (Washington, D.C.: Brookings Institution, 1984).

3. Milton Friedman, "General Revenue, Yes; Payroll Taxes, No!" in *The Crisis in Social Security*, ed. M. Boskin.

4. See R. Burkhauser and K. Holden, *A Challenge to Social Security: The Changing Roles of Women and Men in American Society* (New York: Academic Press, 1982) and R. Ricardo-Campbell, *Social Security: A Mature System in an Aging Society* (Palo Alto, Calif.: Hoover Institution Press, 1983) for significant contributions to the debate over the appropriate treatment of men and women under Social Security. I have learned much from the work of these authors.

5. See P. Ferrara, *Social Security Reform: The Family Plan* (Washington, D.C.: Heritage Foundation, 1982).

6. See M. Feldstein, "The Social Security Funded National Capital Accumulation," in *Funding Pensions: The Issues and Implications* for *Financial Markets* (Boston: Federal Reserve Bank of Boston, 1977).

7. Interfund "borrowing" was used to shore up the OASDI in the early 1980s.

Index

Administration of Social Security, 81–82, 144, 146
Administrative cost, 74–75, 81–82
Age
   and benefits, 84–86, 113–14, 120–22, 151, 158–59, 165–68, 175; *see also* Elegibility age for full benefits
   and population, 2; *see also* Demographic forecasting
   at retirement, 11, 13, 46, 49–50, 59, 61; *see also* Early retirement
   and taxes, 133–35, 150, 158,
Aged; *see* Elderly
Aged support ratio, 39–40
Agricultural employment, 56
AIME; *see* Average indexed monthly earnings
Allocation of resources; *see* Resource allocation
Annuities, 6, 7, 72, 81, 101–2, 128, 143; *see also* Benefits, as annuities
   actuarially fair, 68, 86, 94, 104, 117, 131, 170
   in two-tier system, 86–87, 115–18, 122–23, 140–41, 146–47
Australia, 5
Austria, 131
Average indexed monthly earnings (AIME), 112, 118, 120, 143, 150, 174–75
Average monthly earnings (AME), 174–75
Avrin, Marcy, 35

Baby boom generation, 2, 48, 63, 96–97, 99
   effect on Social Security, 15–16, 39–40, 46, 89–91, 120, 135–36, 158–59
Barro, Robert, 77–79
Benefit formula, 75, 82, 146, 174–75
   changes in, 106–7, 112–13, 115, 140, 143
   inequities in, 84–86, 99, 110, 120
Benefit projections, 89, 133–34
Benefits, 3–4, 31–32, 49, 55, 60–62, 66, 69, 79, 127, 175–81; *see also* Delayed retirement credit; Means test; Social adequacy program; *types of benefits; and benefits under subjects*
   as annuities, 14, 19, 29, 73, 83
   financing of, 94–100, 126; *see also* Payroll tax; Tax revenues; *and* Trust fund
   increases in, 2, 9, 44, 63, 103–4
   reduction of, 11, 90, 109–10, 119–20, 129, 141
   taxation of, 11, 85n, 106–8, 114–15, 150
   as transfer payments, 150–51, 158–59, 165
Bequests, 77–78
Birth rate; *see* Fertility rate
Blacks, 51
Bonds, 101–2
Boskin, Michael, J., 35, 60–62, 86, 89, 106, 108
Budget, 3, 127, 131–32, 135; *see also* Public spending